V

Wilfred Burchett

Verso

Shadows of Hiroshima

Verso Editions and NLB
15 Greek Street, London W1

Filmset in Plantin by
Comset Graphic Designs

Printed by
The Thetford Press Ltd,
Thetford, Norfolk

ISBN 0 86091 080 6
      0 86091 783 5 (Pbk)

Contents

Preface

Why write a book thirty-eight years after an event? Readers have often asked why I did not tackle the task earlier due to my unique experience of being the first Western journalist in Hiroshima after the Atomic Bomb. There are many reasons, including the fact that within days of having written what I only later understood was an historic dispatch from the nuclear-stricken city, I was transferred to Europe and from there to innumerable other international hot spots. It was not until 1971, a quarter of a century after the first nuclear war was unleashed against human beings, that I returned to Hiroshima.

This was in a period when world attention was focused on the 'conventional' (although no less genocidal) warfare in Indochina and when the dangers of nuclear war seemed to have receded, temporarily, into the background. Also I had assumed—most mistakenly—that what had happened in Hiroshima on 6 August 1945 and its aftermath had been so well documented and reported that there was nothing new to add to the subject. It was only when the appalling threat of nuclear war again loomed on the horizon, reinforced by a complacency about the effects of such a holocaust which was based, in turn, (as I discovered to my shock) on ignorance as to what had happened at Hiroshima and Nagasaki, that I felt it was high time to record my own experiences in detail.

Visiting Hiroshima repeatedly in the decade since 1971, investigating the fate of the survivors and studying everything relevant that I could find on the subject, I arrived at the conclusion that I had previously failed to grasp the full extent of the crimes committed there and at Nagasaki. In particular, I had greatly underestimated the extent and persistence of the official cover-up of the reasons for dropping the bombs and of the long-term effects on survivors.

In my view, it has become urgent—virtually a matter of life or death—for people today to understand what really did happen in Hiroshima nearly forty years ago. Once again we all face the actual risk of being consumed by the same nightmarish blast, inferno and radioactive shroud that killed almost half of that city's population back in 1945.

Splashed across the front page of the London *Daily Express* under which my original report from Hiroshima was first published was the sub-heading: 'I Write This As A Warning To The World'. Obviously I could little imagine at the time that the bombs which wiped out Hiroshima and Nagasaki—totally dwarfing the aerial blitzes of the rest of the Second World War—would soon seem puny in their destructive power compared to the capacity of thermonuclear strategic weapons to wipe out entire societies. Indeed the doomsday arsenals of the present cold war build-up might erase human culture, if not the earth's biosphere itself. The danger is therefore absolute.

Dr Jerome Weisner, chief science adviser to several American presidents and former head of the Massachusetts Institute of Technology, reacted as follows to President Reagan's 'Star Wars' announcement of 23 March 1983: 'Most technical people doubt that anti-nuclear devices in space will work, but if they do, it's wishful thinking to believe they would provide impenetrable defences. There are ten thousand or more nuclear weapons on each side. A defence system that would knock out 90-95 per cent would be a miracle—and the remaining 5-10 per cent would be enough to totally destroy civilization. ...'[1] Other experts have estimated that the present stocks of nuclear weapons are sufficient to destroy the world *thirteen* times over and the megatonnage is constantly being improved.

We are constantly being reassured by Western leaders that the actual threat is minimal—so long, that is, as we continue to provide them with a blank cheque for the build-up of even more apocalyptic nuclear weapons systems under the sea and in outer space. They pursue the chimera of restoring the absolute nuclear superiority they briefly possessed at the end of the Second World War, in the deadly delusion that this would allow them to dictate the course of history and to dam the tide of social change. Moreover, if the first forty years of the nuclear epoch are precedent, they are lying to us, massively and systematically.

In 1945 I was too overwhelmed by the enormity of what had happened at Hiroshima and Nagasaki to appreciate the cool deliberation and advance planning that went into manufacturing the subsequent cover-up. There was a whole series of questions—so obvious in retrospect—that I failed to ask or piece together at the time: Why, as a well-known and accredited war correspondent, did I encounter such difficulty in transmitting my report to my newspaper? Why did I return to such hostility from American military authorities in Tokyo? Why was I immediately whisked off to a military hospital, if not to isolate me from my colleagues? How did it happen that when I was discharged from the hospital, my Contax camera—containing a full roll of pictures taken in Hiroshima —was stolen? Why did General MacArthur want to expel me from Japan?

At the time I put most of these incidents down to the mysterious behaviour of war-time bureaucracies. Later I was forced to suspect more sinister explanations. Ineluctably, as I learned of the experiences of journalist contemporaries and Japanese survivors, I was forced to recognize the existence of an official policy to suppress accurate reportage of the terrible after-effects of nuclear war. This cover-up—which continues today—is closely related to other attempts to disguise the reasons why President Truman decided to drop two atomic bombs on an already prostrated and defeated Japan. The total accumulation of lies, half-truths and manipulated public opinion, at the ultimate expense of hundreds of thousands of lives (including Americans as well as Japanese), makes the Watergate Affair look like rather small change.

If the threat of nuclear war has become the central issue of our time, precipitating an international peace movement that cuts across all geographical and ideological boundaries, then it is my clear duty, based on my own special experiences to add this contribution to our collective knowledge and consciousness. With apologies that it has been so delayed.

1

The First Nuclear War

On 11 August 1945, the Swiss Legation in Tokyo, which looked after American interests in Japan, forwarded the following memorandum to the US State Department. The contents were released twenty-five years later:

> The Legation of Switzerland in charge of Japanese interests has received an urgent cable from the authorities abroad, requesting that the Department of State be immediately apprised of the following communication from the Japanese Government reading, in translation, as follows:
>
> On 6 August 1945, American airplanes released on the residential district of the town of Hiroshima, bombs of a new type, killing and injuring in one second a large number of civilians and destroying a great part of the town. Not only is the city of Hiroshima a provincial town without any protection or special military installations of any kind, but also none of the neighbouring region of this town constitutes a military objective.[2]
>
> In a declaration President Truman has asserted that he would use these bombs for the destruction of docks, factories and installations for transportation.[3] However, this bomb, provided with a parachute, in falling has a destructive force of great scope as a result of its explosion in the air. It is evident, therefore, that it is technically impossible to limit the effect of its use to special objectives such as designated by President Truman, and the American authorities are perfectly well aware of this. In fact, it has been established on-the-scene that the damage extends over a great area and that combatant and non-combatant men and women, old and young, are massacred without discrimination by the atmospheric pressure of the explo-

sion, as well as by the radiating heat which results therefrom. Consequently there is involved a bomb having the most cruel effects humanity has ever known, not only as far as the extensive and immense damage is concerned, but also for reasons of suffering endured by each victim.

It is an elementary principle of international public law that in time of war the belligerents do not have unlimited right in the choice of attack and that they cannot resort to projectile arms or any other means capable of causing the enemy needless suffering... The bombs in question, used by the Americans, by their cruelty and by their terrorizing effects, surpass by far gas or any other arm, the use of which is prohibited....

The Americans have effected bombardments of towns in the greatest part of Japanese territory, without discrimination massacring a great number of old people, women and children, destroying and burning down Shinto and Buddhist temples, schools, hospitals, living quarters, etc. This fact alone means that they have shown complete defiance of the essential principles of humanitarian laws, as well as international law. They now use this new bomb, having an uncontrollable and cruel effect much greater than any other arms or projectiles ever used to date. This constitutes a new crime against humanity and civilization. The government of Japan, in its own name and at the same time in the name of all of humanity and civilization, accuses the American Government with the present Note of an inhuman weapon of this nature, and demands energetically, abstinence from its use.

It is obvious that this document was drafted before 9 August when a second A-bomb destroyed Nagasaki. Translation and transmission delays account for it being delivered in Washington only on 11 August. The State Department was in a quandary. It could ignore a direct protest from the Japanese Government, but not a memorandum from the Swiss Government. The latter was handed over to the Special War Problems Division which in turn passed it on to the State-War-Navy Coordinating Committee, where it was discussed on 5 September 1945. The following is the result of their deliberations:

Problem: Should a reply be made to this Japanese protest? If so, what should be the nature of the reply?

Recommendations:
(1) That the receipt of the Swiss Memorandum be merely acknowledged.
(2) That no reply to this Japanese protest should be made in view of the events that have transpired since the receipt of this note from the Swiss Legation.
(3) *That no publicity whatsoever be given to the receipt of this protest from the Japanese Government.*

On 24 September this recommendation was accepted by the State-War-Navy Coordinating Committee and on 24 October—six weeks after the Swiss memorandum was received—the State Department sent the following reply:

The Department of State acknowledges the receipt of a Memorandum dated 11 August 1945 from the Legation of Switzerland in charge of Japanese interests in the United States with the exception of the Territory of Hawaii, transmitting the text of a communication from the Japanese Government concerning the *alleged* [author's emphasis] bombing on 6 August 1945 of the town of Hiroshima by United States airplanes.[4]

Why would the State Department cover itself with possible ridicule by referring to an alleged bombing of Hiroshima? Why six weeks of deliberations before a reply was made? And why hide the whole incident from public gaze for a quarter of a century? Because the Japanese government's account of what had happened to human beings, moderate as it was, ran counter to Washington's decision to stress only the enormous destructive power of the Bomb against material objectives while attempting to cover up what it did to human victims. I still find it difficult to accept that American nuclear war planners had sufficient foresight to envisage world-wide public reaction decades later when it became clear that they were planning the ultimate horror of an all-out nuclear war. But the facts are there and form part of an established pattern. Such a cover-up policy was later applied to American troops who died from the effects of nuclear tests in the Nevada desert and even to animals killed by nuclear radiation near the testing ranges. As far as the livestock is concerned, there was a revealing report in the

International Herald Tribune (Paris) on 8 August 1982. Under the
headline: JUDGE CITES US DECEIT IN FALLOUT TRIAL, the report
from Salt Lake City ran as follows:

> A federal district judge has declared that the US government
> deliberately concealed evidence, pressured witnesses and engaged
> in deceitful conduct in a 1956 trial over whether thousands of sheep
> died from radioactive fallout. In that trial, a group of Utah sheep
> ranchers sought unsuccessfully to prove that their animals' deaths
> were linked to above-ground atomic tests. ... Judge A. Sherman
> Christiansen, who ruled in favour of the government twenty-six
> years ago, vacated his decision and ordered a new trial on behalf of
> the ranchers who, since 1953, have been seeking legal compensa-
> tion for the loss of more than four thousand sheep.
>
> In what legal experts characterize as a rare finding, Judge Chris-
> tiansen concluded that the government had 'perpetrated a fraud
> upon the court'. He said that in the original trial government
> witnesses and officials had made intentionally false and deceptive
> representations, attempted to pressure witnesses not to testify about
> their real opinions, intentionally withheld information in a manner
> that was misleading and deceitful, and answered questions in a
> deceptive fashion.
>
> Judge Christiansen said he was not now ruling that radioactive
> fallout contributed to the death of the sheep, but rather that
> because of a government deception he did not have adequate
> evidence to make a proper ruling in 1956... In addition to the sheep
> case, arguments are to begin in the Federal District Court here next
> month on a 4-year-old lawsuit in which 900 Utah residents are
> seeking damages on behalf of themselves or family members who
> have contracted illnesses, including cancer, that they say were caus-
> ed by fallout. Also scores of soldiers who were assigned to the
> Nevada test site have also been seeking compensation from
> Congress.

The thirty-seven years between the original Japanese protest and
the case of the Nevada sheep have been marked by lies and deceit
of monstrous proportions from the highest levels of US policy-
makers. I was unwittingly caught up in the early stages of the
cover-up operation designed to hide what happens to animate beings exposed even to the relatively 'midget' bombs such as those

exploded at Hiroshima, Nagasaki and during the early tests in the Nevada desert. My insistence on trying to establish the facts led to my first major confrontation with the top-level information pedlars of the US government. It is a battle that has continued almost uninterruptedly ever since. As the first Allied journalist to reach Hiroshima, I was unaware of what I was getting into, although obviously I would have reported as I did in any case.

In a Chronology appended to what is by far the most complete account of what happened at Hiroshima and Nagasaki—and the consequences—one finds the following entries:[5]

> *3 September 1945*: Meeting on A-bomb disease held in Hiroshima, with lectures given by Masao Tsuzuki and Masashi Miyake.[6]
> Occupation press corps enters Hiroshima. Australian journalist Wilfred Burchett enters Hiroshima independently, cables story on local situation.
> *6 September*: Journalist George Wyler enters Nagasaki to gather information.[7]
> *9 September*: Special Manhattan Enginering District Investigating Group conducts survey of Hiroshima.
> *12 September*: Group head, T. Farrell denies newspaper reports on biological sterility (press release Tokyo).

I could have had no idea when I entered Hiroshima just four weeks after the city's incineration that this would become a watershed in my life, decisively influencing my whole professional career and world outlook. The 'Occupation press corps' referred to in the Chronology was a group of hand-picked American journalists flown out directly from Washington to report on the devastating power of America's new war-winning weapon. They were selected on the basis of their prestige, credibility or expert knowledge to participate in a great cover-up conspiracy, although some of them may not have realized this at the time. They had been assured that they would be the first foreign journalists to enter Hiroshima—well ahead of their war correspondent colleagues who had covered the long and dangerous island-hopping operations and jungle battlefields which paved the way to Japan's defeat. A few were also veteran war correspondents, but the majority were being rewarded for faithful rewrites of the Washington headquarters' communiqués. In view of their officially guaranteed 'scoop', they were chagrined to find an Australian rival wandering around in the Hiroshima rubble when they arrived.

The high-level public relations officers who were carefully shepherding them treated me with suspicion and hostility. Who was I and how did I get there? Their hostility seemed disproportionate to the usual frustrations of professional competition. My journey to Hiroshima—as will be related later—had been tough and dangerous, but my request for a lift back to Tokyo with their special US Army plane was curtly refused. As was also my plea that they at least take a copy of my report to pass on to my *Daily Express* colleague at press headquarters. At the time I put this down to an excess of zeal by the senior press officer because he had not been able to keep the promise that 'his' journalists would be the first to report from Hiroshima. (I learned later that some of his charges—colleagues from war reporting in the Pacific—protested at the cavalier way in which I was treated.) If the refusal to carry back my report was only an excess of zeal, I could afford to smile inwardly. By the time of our meeting and unknown to them, my report was being tapped out, letter by letter on a Morse hand-set from Hiroshima to Tokyo. But there was no certainty as to when it would arrive. And I had no inkling that in writing what I did, I was taking on the US military and political establishment.

The most prestigious member of the US journalist delegation was William L. Laurence, for many years the science writer for *The New York Times*. At the time of his Hiroshima visit, he was wearing two hats: one for *The New York Times*, the other as a member of the inner circle of the government's nuclear weapons directorate. Although at the time his favoured official connections were obvious, few of his fellow journalists, much less his millions of readers, were aware of his real plenipotentiary status as the US War Department's nuclear propagandist. Three months before Hiroshima he had been recruited by General Leslie R. Groves, the commander of the Manhattan Project, to act as a super public relations officer and news 'manager'. Given years of voluntary press censorship of any mention of atomic energy, and the general scientific ignorance of most wartime journalists, Laurence—precisely as

Groves had intended—became a virtual oracle for Allied reporters. He alone had access to the Manhattan Project's supersecret plants and laboratories, and had been the sole journalist to observe the Alamogordo test of the prototype A-bomb used against Hiroshima. He had written the famous statement 'from the President' announcing the destruction of Hiroshima, which Truman's Assistant Press Secretary Eban Ayers had read to astonished journalists on the morning of 6 August. His *New York Times* background pieces on the dawn of the nuclear era were syndicated worldwide, and on the morning of 10 August he flew in one of the three bombers which dropped 'Fat Man', the plutonium-fuelled bomb, on Nagasaki.[8] For these deeds, and his exultant descriptions of the 'awesome beauty' of atomic genocide, Laurence later received both a Pulitzer Prize and a War Department commendation.

Laurence's arrival at Hiroshima, in the company of the Manhattan Project's deputy-commander, Brigadier-General Thomas D. Farrell, and the select party of housetrained reporters, was undoubtedly intended as a culminating coup in the official management of what had been described as 'the biggest news story in the history of the world'. It had not been anticipated that a maverick reporter, unvetted by the US War Department or Project Manhattan, would have found the means to arrive at the dead city ahead of the Farrell party. Under these circumstances, and given the pre-rehearsed character of the Investigatory (sic) Group's 'findings', it is no wonder that Laurence in *The New York Times*, and myself in the London *Daily Express* ended up writing diametrically different reports. I reported what I had seen and heard, while Laurence sent back a prefabricated report reflecting the 'official line'.

Hiroshima Dispatch

THE ATOMIC PLAGUE: thus ran the *Daily Express* headline introducing my Hiroshima dispatch. The term 'atomic radiation' was unknown to me—and most readers—at the time. But I knew that some terrible new malady had stricken the survivors of the original blast and fiery holocaust. I had seen some of them in what remained of a hospital and talked to the doctor in charge. The report took up most of the front page and the large part of an inside page of the 5 September 1945 edition. Laurence meanwhile preferred to take refuge behind Farrell. His first report in *The New York Times* appeared, unaccountably, only on 13 September under the following headlines:

No Radioactivity In Hiroshima Ruin

Army Investigators Also Report Absence Of Ground Fusing—68,000 Buildings Damaged

By W.H. Laurence (Wireless to The New York Times)

Datelined Tokyo, 12 September, his report starts:

> Brig. Gen. T.F. Farrell, chief of the War Department's atomic bomb mission, reported tonight after a survey of blasted Hiroshima that the explosive power of the secret weapon was greater even than its inventors envisaged, but he denied categorically that it produced a dangerous, lingering radioactivity in the ruins of the town, or caused a form of poison gas at the moment of explosion...
>
> He said his group of scientists found no evidence of continuing radioactivity in the blasted area on Sept. 9, when they began their investigations and said it was his opinion that there was no danger to be encountered by living in the area at present...
>
> 'The physical destruction in the target area was practically complete,' he reported. 'The scene was one of utter devastation. The total number of destroyed and damaged buildings was 68,000 or somewhere between 80 and 100 per cent of all buildings in the city...'

Another Laurence report from the Alamogordo test site where the first A-bomb exploded had appeared in *The New York Times* the day prior to that from Hiroshima. It was in relation to that report that *The New York Times* revealed that Laurence was serving as a 'special consultant' to the Manhattan Engineering District, the War Department's special service for atomic development. His Alamogordo dispatch was headlined:

US **Atom Bomb Site Belies Tokyo Tales**
by William L. Laurence

ATOM BOMB RANGE, New Mexico, Sept. 9 (delayed)—This historic ground in New Mexico, scene of the first atomic explosion on earth and cradle of a new era in civilization, gave the most effective answer to Japanese propaganda that radiations were responsible for deaths even the day after the explosion, Aug. 6, and that persons entering Hiroshima had contracted mysterious maladies due to persistent radioactivity.

To give the lie to these claims, the Army opened the closely-guarded gates of this area for the first time to a group of newspaper men and photographers to witness for themselves the readings on radiation metres carried by a group of radiologists and to listen to the expert testimony of several of the leading scientists who have been intimately connected with the atomic bomb project.

The ground, visited for the first time by Maj. Gen. Leslie R. Groves, overall director of the atomic bomb project, since that historic morning on Monday, July 16, gave awesome testimony on a number of subjects....

Having proved, at least to Laurence's satisfaction that there was no radioactivity at the testing range where the A-bomb was denonated from a steel tower only 100 feet above ground, there was far less likelihood of any at Hiroshima or Nagasaki where, according to Laurence, the bombs were exploded at almost twenty times that altitude. He continued:

This finding is borne out by a report just received by General Thomas F. Farrell, his next in command, who is now in Japan with a group of American scientists to study the effects of the bomb, on the scene.

The studies of the American scientists are still in the preliminary stage, General Groves stated. But, he added that, according to General Farrell, Japanese sources now admitted that eleven days after the bomb had pulverized Hiroshima, the radiation there was much less than the tolerance dose which means, he added, 'that you could live there forever.'

'The Japanese claim', General Groves added, 'that people died from radiation. If this is true, the number was very small.

However, any deaths from gamma rays were due to those emitted during the explosion, not to the radiations present afterwards. While many people were killed, many lives were saved, particularly American lives. It ended the war sooner. It was the final punch that knocked them out.'

'The Japanese are still continuing their propaganda aimed at creating the impression that we won the war unfairly and thus attempting to create sympathy for themselves and (obtain) milder terms, an examination of their present statements reveal.'[9]

Like the fumbling and procrastination in replying to the Swiss Government's memorandum, there is something fishy about the correlation of dates in the activities of Farrell and Laurence. Why did Laurence not file his own report from Hiroshima, or at least from Tokyo, where he presumably arrived back from the massacred city on 3 September, or at latest the following morning? He had been in Hiroshima with the other correspondents on the same day as myself. Why the belated story from the atomic range?

Delay on a newspaper dispatch normally means a problem of transmission. It is hard to believe that the telephone lines and telegraph wires were not working between New Mexico and New York. And, in a story filed from Los Alamos on 9 September, how was it possible that General Groves was able to quote Farrell for an on-the-spot report when Farrell only left for Hiroshima on that day, returning to Tokyo three days later? Above all, why the enormous effort to deceive the public into believing that there was no residual radioactivity in the A-bombed cities? With all modesty, I believe that I was partly the cause of all this.

When I stumbled out of a train at Tokyo station on the morning of 7 Sept., after my harrowing journey to Hiroshima and back, my only thought was to get to a hotel and sleep in a bed for the first time in five days.

My return journey had been arduous, to say the least. At Kyoto station—about half way in train-time those days between Tokyo and Hiroshima—I met some Australian POWs, pale ghosts of men who recognized by my suntan and general fitness that I was not one of them. When they realized that I was tangible confirmation

of what had been rumours until then—that the war was really over
—they begged me to leave the train, come to their camp, just show
myself and tell their fellow POWs that the war was over and they
would soon be on their way home. Our mates are dying every
hour, they said. They've only got to see you and hear what you've
told us and you'll save many lives.

I could not refuse despite the notes for follow-up stories on
Hiroshima that were burning holes in my pocket. First I checked
with the Kyoto branch of *Domei* (then the official Japanese news
agency) to learn whether my report had got through to Tokyo. It
was the *Domei* correspondent in Hiroshima who had tapped it out
on his hand Morse set. A beaming employee confirmed that it had
been received in the *Domei* office, then transferred to a *Daily
Express* colleague. For the next few days and nights—I have never
been able to work out how many—I toured all the POW camps in
the Kyoto-Tsuruga area. My message was that the war was really
over, a brief resume of how the end had come, and that they
should hang on for a few more days until arrangements were completed to free them and send them homeward.

An enthusiastic Japanese-speaking American POW said I must
carry the same message to a big, mixed camp at Kobe-Osaka,
where I soon had the local mayor on the mat, pledging to improve
camp conditions immediately—a pledge I extracted from commanders of the half dozen other camps I visited. With a .45 calibre
pistol—loaned me by my *Daily Express* colleague who had arrived
with General MacArthur's forces in Yokohama—strapped to my
waist, I pretended to be an emissary sent by General MacArthur
to ensure that the surrender conditions were being implemented.

Finally I arrived back at Tokyo station, clothes stiff with sweat,
unwashed, unshaven, eyes red with train cinders and lack of sleep.
When I had left Tokyo station what seemed ages ago, the capital
had not yet been occupied. MacArthur's forces were concentrated
in Yokohama, and Tokyo was about to be declared 'off limits'.
Now it was full of smartly dressed American officers and troops.
As I started to slink away from the station to the Dai Ichi Hotel
where I had illegally (although I did not know it at the time) spent
a night making arrangements to get to Hiroshima, a colleague hail-

ed me—very dapper in his freshly-pressed war correspondent's uniform. 'Burchett,' he shouted, 'you've just made it. Come with me to the Imperial Hotel. The top brass are giving a special briefing on Hiroshima.'

'Impossible in the state I'm in,' I replied. 'All I want is a bath and a bed.' 'But,' he argued, 'the briefing is especially to deny your story about radiation sickness in Hiroshima.' So I went. But on the way I learned that the *Daily Express* had not only 'front-paged' my story but had made it available world-wide *gratis*. The American nuclear big shots were furious.

The conference was nearly over when I arrived, but it was clear that its main purpose was to deny my dispatch from Hiroshima that people were dying from the after-effects of the bomb. A scientist in brigadier-general's uniform explained that there could be no question of atomic radiation or the symptoms I had described, since the bombs had been exploded at such a height as to avoid any risk of 'residual radiation'.[10]

There was a dramatic moment as I rose to my feet, feeling that my scruffiness put me at a disadvantage with the elegantly uniformed and bemedalled officers. My first question was whether the briefing officer had been to Hiroshima. He had not. I then described what I had seen and asked for explanations. He was very polite at first, a scientist explaining things to a layman. Those I had seen in the hospital were victims of blast and burn, normal after any big explosion. Apparently the Japanese doctors were incompetent to handle them, or lacked the right medication. He discounted the allegation that any who had not been in the city at the time of the blast were later affected. Eventually the exchanges narrowed down to my asking how he explained the fish still dying when they entered a stream running through the centre of the city. 'Obviously they were killed by the blast or overheated water.'
'Still there a month later?'
'It's a tidal river, so they could be washed back and forth.'
'But I was taken to a spot in the city outskirts and watched live fish turning their stomachs upwards as they entered a certain stretch of the river. After that they were dead within seconds.'
The spokesman looked pained. 'I'm afraid you've fallen victim to

Japanese propaganda,' he said, and sat down. The customary 'Thank you' was pronounced and the conference was ended. Although my radiation story was denied, Hiroshima was immediately put out of bounds, and I was whisked off to a US Army hospital for tests, which showed that my white corpuscle count was down.

The press corps picked this up and I soon received a gentle, admonitory cable from *Daily Express* foreign editor, Charles Foley, to the effect that the paper hoped they would not be scooped by rivals about my own disintegration. The drop in my white corpuscle count was written off by the hospital authorities as due to a knee infection which had been treated by antibiotics. Only later did I learn that the knee infection should have increased the number of white corpuscles battling against the infection on my behalf. A falling-off in white corpuscles, on the other hand, is a typical phenomenon of radiation sickness. By the time I left the hospital I found that my camera, with the historic pictures from Hiroshima still tucked away in its intestines, was missing; that General MacArthur had withdrawn my press accreditation; and that I was to be expelled from Japan for having gone 'beyond the boundaries of "his" occupation zone without permission'. Later, I was to learn of a restriction placed on all Allied journalists seemingly as a direct result of my 'misdemeanours'.

On the day following the transmission of my Hiroshima dispatch from the Yokohama press headquarters, the following report was filed to *The New York Times*.

Yokohama, Japan, Sept. 5. (By wireless to *The New York Times*) As units of the United States (Dismounted) Cavalry Division prepared for entry into Tokyo, Saturday, orders were repeated and enforced today for the withdrawal of all correspondents from the capital.

When a correspondent asked the reason for this step, a spokesman for Gen. Douglas MacArthur replied: 'It is not military policy for correspondents to spearhead the occupation.' Meanwhile general officers and other personnel from Allied Headquarters entered the city today to investigate the hotels where correspondents had been staying. These hotels will be taken over by headquarters which then will assign a hotel that was described by former Tokyo residents as third-rate. News from Japan's capital and news centre now is being filed abroad entirely by the Japanese news agency *Damei*, while American correspondents are forced to remain on routine assignments a mile outside the city limits...

Forced to remain in Yokohama, correspondents belatedly receive handouts of translations from the Japanese press that are carefully edited and selected with a view to upholding the official Japanese line that: 'We were defeated but we hope the Americans will be as good winners as we were losers....'

As we will see later there was method in this seeming MacArthur madness. The concentration of Allied newsmen into a sort of press ghetto and making them dependent on Japanese sources for all significant developments was preparatory to placing a total ban on Japanese journalists or scientists making any reports whatsoever about the fate of A-bomb survivors in Hiroshima or Nagasaki.

2
'A Warning to the World'

How I came to be in Hiroshima, what I saw there and how my report appeared in the *Daily Express* two days after my visit, is a long and complicated story. Parts of it have been mentioned in several previous books and it has been the subject of a number of films made in England, Australia, Italy, Japan, Sweden and elsewhere. It was not until many years after the event, while doing some research for one of these films, that I became aware of the actual consternation that my unauthorized reportage from Hiroshima had caused among the nuclear war zealots in Washington. I had gone to Hiroshima in obedience to the most fundamental and categorial imperative of journalism: Get to the spot as soon as you can, preferably ahead of your colleagues, and faithfully report back to your readers what you have seen and felt. That the other six hundred Allied journalists who had swarmed into Japan considered the surrender-signing ceremony on the battleship *Missouri* to be the most earth-shaking event at the moment was their affair. Their minds were on the past, mine on the future. I doubt that anyone reads today the dramatic and colourful accounts they wrote of the surrender, even those from the pens of some of the Western world's most illustrious journalists.

I had joined the *Daily Express* while covering Japan's war against China. Thus I happened to be in the Chinese wartime capital of Chungking—then the world's most bombed city—when Japan attacked Pearl Harbour, destroying the battleships of the United States Pacific Fleet. From then until the end of 1943, I was accredited to the China-Burma-India (CBI) Command. My first assignment was to cover the Japanese rout of the British from Burma and the unsuccessful counter-attack from India to regain a foothold in southwest Burma. Known as the Arakan campaign, the result for me personally was four months in hospital recovering from a strafing by a Japanese fighter plane. That was symbolic of the inglorious fate of the campaign as a whole.

By the end of 1942, the Soviet Army had stopped the Nazis at Stalingrad and the Western Allies had finally opened a long-awaited and oft-postponed Second Front in Italy. With Hitler's armies on the retreat in Russia and an Allied toe-hold in the West, complete victory over the Axis forces in Europe seemed only a matter of time. Thus the military strategists and Fleet Street editors started looking East. Japan, having captured all the ports and major industrial centres of China, as well as occupying raw-material-rich Southeast Asia, was seemingly in a very formidable position. The colonial armies of Britain, France and Holland had been easily defeated, while MacArthur had narrowly averted capture with the collapse of American resistance in the Philippines. Moreover, to defend their newly created imperium—the notorious 'Co-prosperity Sphere'—the Japanese had transformed strategic islands in the Central Pacific into a string of powerful naval and air bases.

The bold concept of US Admiral Nimitz, once his fleet had been reconstituted and vastly expanded, was to drive out the Japanese and turn these islands into steppingstones to set American forces ashore on Japan. 'Strike at the heart' was the formula often used. Meanwhile MacArthur was supposed to drive the Japanese out of New Guinea—the southernmost position of their drive towards Australia—then to advance through the large island masses of Indonesia and especially the Philippines towards Japan from the South. (Greatest credit for stopping and then driving back the Japanese from New Guinea goes to Australian troops, who fought some of the epic battles of the whole Pacific campaign.) The grand strategy envisioned an eventual junction between the forces of Nimitz advancing from the East and those of MacArthur advancing from the South, concentrating a vast armada and landing force for the expected costly assault on Japan itself.

Because of bureaucratic delays with my accreditation, I missed the first of the island-hopping operations—against the Gilbert Islands, some 2,400 miles southwest of Pearl Harbour. It was almost a disaster. Someone on the planning side had misjudged the tides. Landing-craft were hung up on the coral reef and man-built obstacles because the attack took place at low tide. The Japanese massacred the first assault waves with automatic weapons. It was an error never repeated.

For the next eighteen months, I alternated between assault landings with the Marines and the support and diversionary operations of the aircraftcarriers. My reporting calendar in this period included the battles for the Marianas and Caroline Islands; the landings at Leyte in the Philippines and the subsequent greatest aero-naval battles in military history, ending with the virtual destruction of the Japanese Fleet; the assault against Iwo Jima; and the carrier-borne strike against Tokyo and other Japanese cities. During the battle for Okinawa—which I reported from the HMS King George V (flagship of a token British contingent)—we faced the full strength of the 'Kamikazes' for the first time. It was an uncanny, awesome sight to see them diving steadily down through what looked like coloured snowstorms of anti-aircraft fire from their intended victims and protective escorts, to explode on their targets in an appallingly high percentage of cases.

Due to the complexity of transferring from a British warship to a comparable American one during the daily battles, and from a ship of the line to a landing craft, I got ashore at Okinawa when the land fighting was almost over. But it was there, while lining up for my hamburgers and mash at a US Army canteen, that I heard snatches of a newscast, in which an excited announcer was talking about an enormously powerful new bomb that had just been dropped on a place called Hiroshima. Above the clatter of tin trays and plates, small talk about the previous night's movie or the Japanese infiltrator someone's unit had just shot, it was impossible to catch the details about the new bomb. As the cook's aide dumped my lunch on to the tray, I asked what the newscast was all about: 'Ah,' he said, 'it's about some great new bomb we've just dropped on the Japs. A lotta good it'll do us here.' And I shuffled on down the line none the wiser. (At the time it was taken for granted that the Okinawa operation which had been so costly—12,000 US troops killed, 36,000 wounded, 34 Allied ships sunk and 368 damaged in almost three months of fighting—would be nothing in terms of human and material losses compared to the final assault on Japan.) In the comparative quiet of an officers' mess that evening, I learned that it was an A-bomb which had been dropped 'on a place called Hiroshima' and I made a mental note that this would be my first goal if I made it to Japan.

I did make it, aboard the USS *Millette*, a freighter transformed into a troop transport, laden with Marines who were to be among the first landing party. Their job was to spike the enemy's guns and ensure security for the first waves of occupation troops. It was in Yokohama and not Tokyo that Henry Keys and I met for the first time since Melbourne. He had flown to Yokohama with an advance party from MacArthur's headquarters. Having picked up a few phrases of Japanese from a US military manual within half an hour of landing at the Yokosuka naval base, I found that trains ran regularly between Yokosuka and Tokyo. Together with Bill McGaffin of the Chicago *Daily News*, an inseparable companion of many battlefields, we were soon on a Tokyo-bound train. Our Japanese fellow-passengers showed surprise, but not hostility. One of them, in good English, indicated at which station we should get out for the Dai Ichi Hotel—not far from the centre of what was left of Tokyo after General LeMay's genocidal fire raids. After a mild altercation with the receptionist at the Dai Ichi, ending in our filling out a tourist-type form concerning 'length of stay', 'home address' and other irrelevancies, we booked in for the night, quickly discovering that cigarettes were an acceptable form of currency.

Next morning, while McGaffin strolled around taking notes for a piece on the atmosphere, I sought out *Domei* (today *Kyodo*), the official Japanese news agency. I was received with professional courtesy by someone on the foreign desk, to whom I explained my most ardent desire to get to Hiroshima as soon as possible and report exactly what had happened there. He gave me a startled look and said: 'But no one goes to Hiroshima. Everyone is dying there.' When I insisted that if this was the case it made my mission all the more urgent, he consulted with some colleagues and said: 'There is a daily train leaving Tokyo at 6 a.m. which stops at Hiroshima. But no one can say at what time it stops there.'

The upshot was that he agreed to buy me a return ticket in exchange for my taking some food and cigarettes to Nakamura-*san*, the *Domei* correspondent in Hiroshima. I asked if there was any chance of getting a message back to their Tokyo office through Nakamura-*san*. He replied: 'It is an odd situation. He has a Morse hand-set and gets messages through to us. But he has no receiving apparatus so we cannot contact him. There are no radios in Hiroshima and the trains are not carrying newspapers there. Somehow he knows we get his messages, so he keeps on filing. If you like, we will give you a letter to Nakamura-*san* and ask him to help you. And please tell him how highly we value his services.'

Back to the Dai Ichi hotel for a rendezvous with Bill McGaffin and the return trip to Yokosuka. McGaffin had come only to cover the *Missouri* surrender ceremony after which he was to return directly to Chicago. So it was no disloyalty to that highly-esteemed friend in not disclosing my secret plan. A friend at the Navy press centre to whom I did divulge my project, delighted at the idea that it might be one of 'their' correspondents who made it first into Hiroshima, provided me with adequate provisions including a huge chunk of beef for my *Domei* contact in Tokyo. All correspondents assembled that evening at a Yokohama hotel, temporarily designated as the Allied press headquarters, and I had an uproarious reunion with my compatriot-colleague, Henry Keys. Predictably there was a brief exchange of the hair-raising experiences we had each been through and—in view of the exceptionally high death-toll of correspondents—miraculously survived. The matter of division of labour for the following days we settled even more rapidly than when we had 'split the Pacific up'. Henry would cover the *Missouri* surrender ceremony and I would do my best to get to Hiroshima. He would do his utmost to maintain contact with *Domei* in Tokyo and in case the dubious miracle worked, would relay my report to London via the Yokohama press centre.

We shared the same room that night, conscious of the necessity of absolute secrecy in relation to our colleagues. Fortunately they were all due to leave very early the following morning to be on the decks of the USS *Missouri* for the ceremony which would officially mark the end of the Second World War. Press officers came to wake us up and were appalled to discover that one of the fold was groaning on his bed with what appeared to be a bad case of diarrhea, his anxious colleague applying warm towels to his stomach. Nothing to be done, but abandon me to miss one of the 'greatest moments of history'. As Henry left to join his colleagues he wished me good luck and, saying: 'You may need this', he thrust a Colt .45 automatic in my hand. He said he had 'souvenired' it from one of the battlefields. I took it reluctantly, together with the webbing belt to which it was attached. War correspondents were not supposed to carry side-arms, but as the war was to be officially ended within a few hours, my scruples were short-lived. I tucked it into my haversack with my Hermes typewriter and provisions.

Less than an hour after the departure of the 'six hundred', I was in *Domei's* Tokyo office, exchanging my chunk of beef for a return ticket to Hiroshima and a precious note to Nakamura-*san*. Precisely at 6 a.m., I was pushed into a terribly over-crowded train by some *Domei* colleagues who fervently expressed their hopes—with some misgivings, I felt—that all would go well.

Ground Zero

One of the most hazardous parts of my venture was spent during the first eight or nine hours—I had been warned that the journey would last from fifteen to thirty hours. The train was overflowing with freshly demobilized troops and officers. The officers still wore their long swords with *samurai* daggers tucked into their belts. They occupied all the passenger compartments, while the ordinary troops were crammed onto the platforms separating the carriages. I had no alternative but to use my elbows and find standing space with them. They did not know what to make of me. I had shoved my very military-looking war correspondent's cap into the knapsack. Wearing marine jungle greens, I clutched an umbrella, hoping it would symbolize my civilian status.

The Japanese GIs, short, weary men, wearing leg putties, were very sullen at first, chattering about me in what I sensed was a hostile way. When I handed round a packet of cigarettes, however, they brightened up. (I was soon to learn that the price of cigarettes had risen ten to twenty-fold since the news of the surrender was known). In return I was offered a few swigs of *saki* with which the troops seemed to have filled their water canteens, and some bits of dried fish and hard-boiled eggs. After the first hour we were wartime buddies. They roared with laughter when I showed them scars around my right knee and a protruding bit of unremoved bullet, received from a Japanese fighter in Burma; I produced my typewriter to show that I was a journalist. Space was found for me to sit on one of the enormous bundles they all had and the *saki* flowed more freely. After demobilization, they had been allowed to help themselves to as much food and drink as they could carry, as well as their weapons—concealed among blankets (but that I discovered only later).

After the first five or six hours, my fellow platform-swingers, ruddy of face, bleary of eyes and glowing with *saki*, started dropping off at the various stops, staggering away with their huge bundles. No salutes, I noted, for officers who got off at the same stops, no bows, no signs of recognition even. I managed to get a place in the seating compartment to which our platform gave access, grimy as I was from smoke and cinders. The hostility was total. An American in priest's clothes whom I approached with exuberance, not entirely due to *saki*, warned me in guarded language that the situation was very tense. Then I noticed that he had an armed escort and was very nervous. He said that a smile or handshake would be taken as gloating over the surrender, which was being signed at about that moment, and could cost us our lives. He warned about those 'with the big sticks between their legs'. He had been brought to Tokyo to broadcast to the Occupation troops as to how they should behave to avoid friction. Now he was being taken back to the camp in which he had been interned since Pearl Harbour.

Bothersome also was that for what seemed about half the time—and that is still the case today—the train plunged into long tunnels. The difference between then and today is that the train was blacked out and there was no lighting in the tunnels. Then we averaged about 40 kilometres per hour, today 220. To be decapitated by a sabre in the dark was not a pleasant prospect but it seemed to me that my new fellow-travellers desired nothing more than to do just that, their hands constantly fumbling with the hilts of their swords and looking daggers at me.

Another problem was to know when I reached Hiroshima—all station signs were written exclusively in Japanese ideographs (today they are duplicated in English). The priest and his escort left the train at Kyoto and he informed me that I was about half way to my journey's end. I had learned from my phrase book that '*Kono eki-wa nanti i meska*' meant: 'What is the name of this station?' This saved me from uttering the name of what then seemed to be the immediate cause of the Japanese surrender. I had no interest in adding new fuel to the fire of the officers' outrage at my presence among them. It was only later that I understood that they were part of what were known as the 'hotheads', ready to defy the emperor and continue the war. They were being bundled out of Tokyo to avoid incidents during the surrender ceremony and the first days of occupation. Seven or eight hours out of Kyoto, I started my ritual question. By that time the officers had thinned out, replaced by civilians. When someone replied: '*Kono eki-wa Hiroshima eki desu*' (This is Hiroshima station) I would leap out. At just 2 a.m., twenty hours after leaving Tokyo, the welcome reply came. The compartment by then was so crammed with sitting and standing passengers that I had to clamber out through the window, my knapsack handed me by my passenger-neighbour.

The station, formerly a brick building, seemed nothing but a roof propped up with poles. A rough barrier had been set up funnelling passengers to two wooden gates at which tickets were collected. As I found later, it was about 2,000 metres from the epicentre (or ground zero as the Americans say) where the Bomb exploded. When I passed through the ticket-control gate, I was grabbed by two black-uniformed, sabre-carrying guards. Assuming I was an escaped POW, they escorted me to an improvised lock-up and made me understand I was not to move. As it was almost twenty-four hours since I had left my Yokohama hotel room and was pitch dark, there was no point in trying to argue. I handed around some cigarettes and drank some hot water, offered with some chick-peas by a woman in the lock-up, settled into a rickety chair and went to sleep. At sun-up I produced my precious letter to Nakamura-*san* and displayed my typewriter, trying to make the point that I was a professional colleague. My status had clearly improved and I was able to stroll over and have a closer look at what was left of the station. After a couple of hours, Mr Nakamura turned up with a Canadian-born young Japanese woman who spoke excellent English.

At this point it is appropriate to pay a tribute to the courage, the integrity and internationalist outlook of Nakamura. He accepted me for what I was: a journalist who wanted to perform his professional duty. From the first moment it was clear that he did not consider me as an enemy. I told him that my concern was not just with the material destruction, the dimensions of which I could measure even from the state of the railway station. What did this monstrous new weapon do to human beings? If he could help me to discover the truth, I would report things as I saw them. He accepted my request at face value and promised to try to transmit whatever I wrote back to *Domei* in Tokyo. He was clearly delighted and moved by the letter I had brought with the confirmation that his reports were getting through and were highly appreciated.

We walked through the flattened rubble of the 68,000 buildings, which Brig. Gen. Thomas Farrell was so proudly to proclaim had been destroyed or damaged, to what was left of the eight-storey Fukuoka department store, on the third floor of which, the survivors of the city's police force had set up their headquarters. The police were extremely hostile and the atmosphere was tense, as Nakamura explained who I was and what I wanted. The more Nakamura explained the more the tension increased. There was some shouting by the police and the interpreter became pale as she

translated my rare interventions. It was only thirty-five years later,
at the *Kyodo* headquarters in Tokyo, that Nakamura explained
what went on. A majority of the police officers were for shooting
all three of us. In the end—of all people—it was the head of the
dreaded 'Thought Control Police,' outranking the others, who
accepted the explanations of Nakamura and myself. 'Show him
what his people have done to us', he said, obviously taking me for
an American. He even arranged a police car to drive me through
the rubble and ruins and on to the Communications Hospital, one
of the city's two hospitals of which enough had survived to render
what aid was possible for the A-bomb victims. (Nakamura, who
seemed hale and hearty in May 1980, died a few months after our
reunion: one of the many who survived the attack and its aftermath, then suddenly died for no apparent reason.)

As to my impressions, I can do no better than repeat them as
they were published in the *Daily Express*, pounded out on my
ancient Baby Hermes, as I sat on a chunk of rubble that had
escaped pulverization at the very centre of the explosion. I packed
as much as possible into that one report, having no guarantee of
getting another chance of instant transmission, and having no idea
what awaited me on my return journey. Apart from some garbles
in transmission and some insertions, apparently by the science
editor, the story is as close to the original as possible. (The carbon
copy of what I wrote disappeared in Tokyo at the same time as my
camera, so I have no other record than what follows.)

> In Hiroshima, thirty days after the first atomic bomb destroyed the
> city and shook the world, people are still dying, mysteriously and
> horribly—people who were uninjured in the cataclysm from an
> unknown something which I can only describe as the atomic
> plague.
> Hiroshima does not look like a bombed city. It looks as if a
> monster steamroller has passed over it and squashed it out of ex-
> istence. I write these facts as dispassionately as I can in the hope
> that they will act as a warning to the world.
> In this first testing ground of the atomic bomb I have seen the most
> terrible and frightening desolation in four years of war. It makes a
> blitzed Pacific island seem like an Eden. The damage is far greater
> than photographs can show.

When you arrive in Hiroshima you can look around for twenty-five and perhaps thirty square miles you can see hardly a building. It gives you an empty feeling in the stomach to see such man-made destruction.

I picked my way to a shack used as a temporary police head-quarters in the middle of the vanished city. Looking south from there I could see about three miles of reddish rubble. That is all the atomic bomb left of dozens of blocks of city streets, of buildings, homes, factories and human beings.

There is just nothing standing except about twenty factory chimneys—chimneys with no factories. A group of half a dozen gutted buildings. And then again nothing.

The police chief of Hiroshima welcomed me eagerly [sic] as the first Allied correspondent to reach the city. With the local manager of *Domei*, the leading Japanese news agency, he drove me through, or perhaps I should say over, the city. And he took me to hospitals where the victims of the bomb are still being treated.

In these hospitals I found people who, when the bomb fell suffered absolutely no injuries, but now are dying from the uncanny after-effects.

For no apparent reasons their health began to fail. They lost appetite. Their hair fell out. Bluish spots appeared on their bodies. And then bleeding began from the ears, nose and mouth.

At first, the doctors told me, they thought these were the symptoms of general debility. They gave their patients Vitamin A injections. The results were horrible. The flesh started rotting away from the hole caused by the injection of the needle. And in every case the victim died.

That is one of the after-effects of the first atomic bomb man ever dropped and I do not want to see any more examples of it.

My nose detected a peculiar odour unlike anything I have ever smelled before. It is something like sulphur, but not quite. I could smell it when I passed a fire that was still smouldering, or at a spot where they were still recovering bodies from the wreckage. But I could also smell it where everything was still deserted.

They believe it is given off by the poisonous gas still issuing from the earth soaked with radioactivity by the split uranium atom.

And so the people of Hiroshima today are walking through the forlorn desolation of their once proud city with gauze masks over their mouths and noses. It probably does not help them physically.

But it helps them mentally.

From the moment that this devastation was loosed upon Hiroshima the people who survived have hated the white man. It is a hate, the intensity of which is almost as frightening as the bomb itself.

The counted dead number 53,000. Another 30,000 are missing which means certainly dead. In the day I have stayed in Hiroshima, 100 people have died from its effects. They were some of the 13,000 seriously injured by the explosion. They have been dying at the rate of 100 a day. And they will probably all die. Another 40,000 were slightly injured.[11] These casualties might not have been as high except for a tragic mistake. The authorities thought this was just another Super-Fort raid. The plane flew over the target and dropped the parachute which carried the bomb to its explosion point. The American plane passed out of sight ... The all-clear was sounded and the people of Hiroshima came out from their shelters. Almost a minute later the bomb reached the 2,000-foot altitude at which it was timed to explode—at the moment when nearly everyone in Hiroshima was in the streets.

This version is quite different from that which Nakamura told me and which I included in my original story. It is possible that Nakamura preferred not to be quoted and omitted his account from that which he transmitted. 'We had an alert early in the morning,' he told me, 'but only two aircraft appeared. We thought they were reconnaissance planes and no one took much notice. The all clear sounded and most people set off for work. Then at 8.20, one plane came back. I was just wheeling out my bicycle to ride to the office when there was a blinding flash—like lightning. At the same time. I felt scorching heat on my face and a tornado-like blast of wind. I fell to the ground and the house collapsed around me. As I hit the ground, there was a booming explosion as if a powerful bomb had burst alongside. When I peered out, there was a tremendous pillar of black smoke, shaped like a parachute, but drifting upward, with a scarlet thread in the middle. As I watched the scarlet core expanded, diffusing through the billowing cloud of smoke until the whole thing was glowing red.

Hiroshima had disappeared and I realized that something new to our experience had occurred. I tried to phone the police and fire brigade to find out what had happened, but it was impossible even to raise the exchange.' None of this precious on-the-spot description from an experienced observer appeared in the *Daily Express*. The published account continued as follows:

> Hundreds upon hundreds of the dead were so badly burned in the terrific heat generated by the bomb that it was not even possible to tell whether they were men or women, old or young.
>
> Of thousands of others, nearer the centre of the explosion, there was no trace. They vanished. The theory in Hiroshima is that the atomic heat was so great that they burned instantly to ashes—except that there were no ashes. If you could see what is left of Hiroshima, you would think that London had not been touched by bombs.
>
> The Imperial palace, once an imposing building is a heap of rubble three feet high, and there is one piece of wall. Roof, floors and everything else is dust ...

(There follows several paragraphs which were obviously inserted by the paper's science editor and which could not possibly have been written by me. Statements like 'almost every Japanese scientist has visited Hiroshima in the past three weeks ...'—In fact the first two scientists had arrived the day before I did and were holding their first meeting at the time I was visiting the Communications Hospital. There is also reference to Nagasaki which I did not visit and so could not have written about, and to the fact that doctors believed the sickness was 'due to radioactivity'. In fact they had no idea what they were trying to cope with.)

An explanation of some inaccuracies and perhaps some omissions from my report comes indirectly from the autobiography of Arthur Christiansen, *Serving My Time*. He was the prestigious editor of the *Daily Express* for many years. Writing of the Hiroshima 'scoop' he remarks that 'poor Peter' (Burchett) was so overcome by the horror of it all that he had to take a hand in editing the story. The science editor clearly wanted to show his erudition on atomic matters, but it was highly unethical to do this under my name.

My only information as to the medical effects from atomic radiation came from Dr Katsube, acting director and chief surgeon of the Communications Hospital, and from the physical aspects of the patients in his hospital Dr Katsube deserves the same credit as Mr Nakamura. He took a great risk in personally escorting me through some of the hospital wards and his descriptions of the symptoms and effects of radiation sickness—although he did not call it that—have stood the test of time. His diagnoses were the more remarkable because there was no medical precedent on which to base them and the hospital was left without any equipment—not even a microscope. Everything had been destroyed in the blast and fiery holocaust which followed.

The reference to 'hatred of the white man' in the *Daily Express* version came from the reactions of the patients and their relatives in the few wards I visited. Patients were laid out on *tatami* (sleeping mats made from woven swamp grass), heads to the wall and groups of family members kneeling around them. (It is a habit in Japan for some member of the family to move into a hospital and feed the patient. But in this case, *only* if family members could stay to perform minimum nursing tasks—changing bandages, keeping their relatives clean, feeding them, etc.—could survivors be admitted. 93 per cent of the city's nurses had been killed or incapacitated in the first seconds of the blast.) I had to see the horrors for myself. I had to look at the suppurating third-degree burns, the bleeding eyes and gums, the fallen-out hair which lay like black haloes around almost every head. The victims and their family members who looked at me with a burning hatred which cut into me like a knife. At one point Dr Katsube spoke to me in English: 'You must go. I cannot be responsible for your life if you stay any longer.' And thus ended my visit to the hospital and my first meeting with Dr Katsube. In fact the general attitude of the Hiroshima citizens in the streets was one of almost total apathy. They were still in a state of trauma. People walked alone or in groups of two or three. No one stopped to speak to anyone else. Even our little group, including a foreigner without a gauze mask, attracted no attention.

Dr Katsube's final words to me were: 'Please report on what

you have seen and ask your people'—he naturally thought I was an American—'to send some specialists who know about this sickness, with the necessary medicines. Otherwise everyone here is doomed to die.'

Despite errors of omission, transmission and insertions, I give great credit to Arthur Christiansen for using my 'warning to the world' in the headlines and for retaining the essential point I wanted to make. Given the elation in the West that the Second World War was now definitely over and that the West had a monopoly of the war-winning weapon demonstrated against Hiroshima and Nagasaki, it was not easy for the editor of Britain's largest circulation daily to deflate the euphoria with such a warning.

3
Covering Up

Never did I imagine that I would be beholden to an officer of the
sinister Japanese Thought Control Police. But it was Officer
Kunihara Dazai who not only saved Nakamura and me from the
wrath of the other police officers, but who escorted us through the
nightmares of the Communications Hospital. Coolly polite,
Officer Dazai (who later became a deputy-minister of Public
Health and Welfare) bowed farewell and left me on my battered
lump of concrete to pound out my report. It was while I was working at ground zero, and while Nakamura was away checking on
train schedules, that the hand-picked American correspondents
arrived. They had flown into Hiroshima airport on a special US
Army transporter which discharged the mini-bus that brought
them to the shattered city. They chatted with me normally until
their officer escorts appeared, then strolled off taking pictures of
the rubble and the grotesquely twisted girders of the few buildings
that had not been melted or pulverized.

To one old acquaintance from some of the island-hopping cam-
paigns, who asked for my impressions, I replied: 'The real story is
in the hospitals.' He shrugged his shoulders and joined the others.
One of their concerns was that fog was closing in and they were
anxious to get back to their plane and take off while there was still
visibility. The one I did not meet that day was Bill Laurence,
although we had rubbed shoulders a few times when we were both
in war correspondent's garb. The massive documentary work by
Japanese scientists, the Chronology of which I have already
referred to accurately recalls the patent disinterest of Laurence and

the other reporters in the fate of the Bomb's victims:

> A group of American reporters who visited Hiroshima on 3 September 1945, expressed satisfaction with the complete destruction of the city. At a press conference held at the prefectural office, *New York Times* reporter, W.L. Laurence noted the total devastation of the city and its population and extolled the obvious superiority of the bomb's potential. Some Japanese reporters present at the press conference raised questions from the standpoint of the bomb's victims. Would Hiroshima be uninhabitable for seventy-five years? Would the atomic bomb contribute to world peace? But Laurence refused to answer such questions. His concern was solely with the might of the bomb, its victims interested him only as proof of that might.
>
> Hiroshima's desolation and the cause of peace were of no interest to him. This singular focus on the atomic bomb's power was not limited to *New York Times* reporter Laurence, it was the policy of the Occupation and the United States Government of that time.[12]

My main worry as Nakamura-*san* escorted me to the train and found me a seat (no officers exerting what had been their automatic privileges less than forty-eight hours earlier) was whether my copy was really on its way to Tokyo and whether Henry Keys would be able to retrieve it. Had I known the real situation my worries would have been greater. No sooner was the surrender ceremony over than MacArthur placed Tokyo out of bounds to Allied personnel. Henry Keys made two attempts to get through from Yokohama but both times he was hauled off the train by US military police at the next stop.

Fortunately for the *Daily Express*, and for me on that occasion, Keys was a very tough, experienced and resourceful journalist, with the sort of pugnacious never-take-no-for-an-answer attitude and total disrespect for officialdom which made Australian journalists very popular among Fleet Street editors.[13] He hired a Japanese journalist to wait in the *Domei* office for a message from Hiroshima, with enough cigarettes and rations to keep him happy. If a message came, he was to rush it immediately to Keys' Yokohama hotel room. Meanwhile, Henry was being grilled by other reporters, especially other Australians working for the

British press, as to my whereabouts. They had all been so thoroughly brainwashed by US Air Corps briefing officers that they accepted their version that the pre-Hiroshima bombings had been so effective that rail and road transport were at a total standstill, with not a single major bridge remaining intact. No one had bothered to check whether this was true or not. They would get to Hiroshima when it suited General MacArthur—by plane, of course—and not before. By putting Tokyo off limits, his press chiefs ensured that no one followed in my footsteps.

Late on the evening of 3 September, the Japanese journalist banged on Henry Keys's door with my copy in his hand. The miracle had worked. Henry retyped it and took it for transmission to the Press Centre. After a quick look at the dateline and subject matter, the duty clerk said: 'This has to pass through censorship, Sir.'

'What censorship?' snarled Henry. 'The war's over and censorship abolished.'

'This is a "special case" Sir, and we can't transmit it.' Henry's toughness came to the surface. Boiling with rage, he fought it out on the spot, and through innumerable phone calls, waking up high-ranking officers and bullying them until someone with high enough authority was glad to yield. Eventually he was led into the telex room and stood over the operator until every word was sent and a confirmatory 'well received' came through from the *Daily Express*.

Farrell and Laurence's group of journalists must have had the shock of their lives. They had left me wandering around the ruins of the Imperial Summer Palace, absolutely certain that it would be at least a full day before I could reach Tokyo. No one else could get there, telegraph and telephone services were out of order, so they had as much time as they liked to write their stories. Morse handsets were antiques and no one imagined that any were functioning in Hiroshima. In view of the hostile attitude of their press officers, I felt under no obligation to enlighten them.

The 600-odd journalists still in Yokohama learned that I had made it only when they were awakened with 'rockets'—the trade term for messages from irate editors whose journalists have been badly beaten on a major story. The reports of the 'select group' which described only material destruction, presenting the A-bomb as just vastly more powerful than conventional ones, were of minor interest compared to the eyewitness description of what it did to human beings. Hence the delay in Laurence's report while the nuclear chiefs and their public relations men fumbled with their gears, eventually deciding to mount a counter-offensive to disprove the existence of radiation sickness or any causes of death other than blast and burns.

In getting my report through I was more fortunate than a colleague, George Weller of the *Chicago Daily News*. I learned of what happened to his reports from Nagasaki only thirty-three years after the event. Passing through Paris where I was then based, he got my telephone number through a mutual friend and called to congratulate me on my Hiroshima exclusive. His newspaper had just ceased publication and he was returning to Chicago from his base in Rome. 'But why now, after so many years?' I asked. 'Because I've never had the chance of talking to you before,' he replied. 'I greatly admired your feat, the more so because you succeeded in doing in Hiroshima what I failed to do in Nagasaki.' As he was just leaving for the airport, there was no chance for us to meet, so I asked for details over the phone and permission to reprint them.

> I covered the *Missouri* surrender ceremony and then set out to do what you did. I knew the authorities were not very keen on this, so I pretended I wanted to visit a little island south of Kyushu (Japan's second largest island where Nagasaki is located) which was the take-off base for the *Kamikaze* pilots. I pretended I wanted to see if any pilots were still there, but found only empty hangars. If I could get any sort of a boat from there and escape the Public Relations 'hawks' I could cross over to Kyushu and take the three hour train journey to Nagasaki. I found a Japanese-speaking American sergeant and confided in him what I wanted to do. 'The war's over, ' he said, 'I'm due to be demobbed. I'll come with you.' We found a little boat and rowed across. We got to Nagasaki and to those hospitals which were still functioning, piecing together a complete analysis. The medical personnel were fully cooperative. I wrote a series of articles, totalling 25,000 words. As a loyal, disciplined

member of the press corps, I sent the material, to MacArthur's press headquarters for clearance and transmission.

I set out on another mission without returning to Tokyo, but slipped on the ship's deck and badly hurt my leg. Eventually I arrived in Guam with my leg in a plaster cast. [Guam was the advanced headquarters of the Pacific Fleet, where correspondents accredited to Admiral Nimitz had permanent billets.] I immediately looked for what I hoped would be congratulatory messages—or at least acknowledgement that my series had arrived. The paper had received nothing. MacArthur had 'killed' the lot. I had always been an enemy of MacArthur's censorship. Now I think he decided to punish me.

He did not suspect what I was only beginning to piece together myself after all the intervening years: that this was part of a pattern of news suppression on a vast scale and in a monstrous cause. As to whether Weller had published the material later, he said: 'No! First of all there were all sorts of other stories I had to cover, but also I had not kept a copy, assuming that it would all be waiting for me in the head office files.'

A few days after MacArthur's expulsion order against me was issued it was rescinded. I had protested that when I left for Hiroshima there was no restriction on correspondents' movements. In any case I was accredited to the American Navy at the time I landed in Yokosuka, and relations between the Army and Navy in those days were at one of their all-time lows. In fact, senior press officers of the Navy were tickled that one of 'their' correspondents had pulled off the Hiroshima scoop and solemnly affirmed that Admiral Nimitz had not issued any orders restricting journalists' activities. Thus I was reprieved. Keys and myself, if we thought of such matters at all those days, would have put the incident over the transmission of my report down to low-level bureaucracy.

On 19 September, following the order referred to earlier restricting the activities of Allied journalists even in Tokyo, draconian restrictions were introduced for Japanese journalists under a new Press Code. Its ten restrictive clauses began as follows (with my emphasis added to the clauses which Japanese journalists later assured me specifically banned reporting on what had happened in Hiroshima and Nagasaki):

(1) News must be strictly according to the truth.
(2) Anything directly or indirectly affecting public security is banned.
(3) Anything not factual must not be reported, *nor anything prejudicial to the armed forces*.
(4) *Anything damaging to the armed forces, anything that would promote hatred or disbelief in the Allied forces, is banned.*

Apparently, only the truth as manifested in Divine Revelation to General MacArthur, purged of any criticism of His armed forces, could be submitted to the gaze of the Japanese public. The new Code went into force immediately.

Through Japanese Eyes

Dismayed by the American authorities' lack of interest in the condition of the A-bomb victims, and by their refusal to share knowledge on the subject with Japanese medical scientists, the Science and Education Bureau of Japan's Ministry of Education set up, together with the country's Scientific Research Council,a 'Special Committee for the Investigation of A-Bomb Damage'. On 21 September, five days after the Committee was established, an advance crew from the Nippon Eiga-sha Film Corporation, commissioned to document the Committee's work, arrived in Hiroshima. Less than a month later, by which time one of the Eiga-sha cameramen had been arrested by Occupation authorities in Nagasaki, the photographing or filming of scenes of A-bomb havoc were banned. On 30 November, the Special Committee presented its first report at Tokyo's Imperial University. On that same day a directive was issued from MacArthur's headquarters requiring any organization to have special permission to conduct research on any matters concerning the effects of the atomic bombing of Hiroshimaor Nagasaki.

At the beginning, all hopes of the Japanese medical and scientific community were based on American aid and expertise. After all, the Americans had built the Bomb, they reasoned, so they must know what the medical effects would be and have developed therapies and medication to deal with the injured. But the days and weeks went by and there were no signs of any help, sympathy or even interest in the fate of the survivors. Dr Michihiko Hachiya, director of the Communications Hospital, kept a diary from 6 August to 30 September. There is an entry on 20 September, which reflected these misplaced hopes. It was shown to me, during a visit to Hiroshima in 1981, by Dr Shigetö, director of the Red Cross and Atom Bomb Victims' Hospital.

After lunch I was dozing on a bed near the window when Mr Sera hastened in, out of breath, and whispered excitedly: '*Sensei*, there's an American officer outside.'

Startled by his words, I was speechless for a moment, and felt fear and anger surge through me. Feelings of hostility got the upper hand and before I had collected my wits I exclaimed in a curt voice;

'Sera-*san*, ignore him!'

'*Sensei*, don't say such things!', he rebuked me and went on excitedly. 'He's at the entrance now. Please see him!'

Gradually, my feelings of hostility gave way to fear and I knew I had no alternative but to see the officer. I was dressed in dirty pants and shirt and, with my mind in the state it was, hardly felt up to confronting the foreigner.

The next moment, I heard steps on the stairs and in walked a dignified, stately officer accompanied by a dark-complexioned guard, wearing a pistol at his side, who assumed the role of interpreter. I informed the pair that I was the director of the Hiroshima Communications Hospital and, after acknowledging each with my eyes, I offered to show them around the wards.

The officer was more interested in the typhoon than the A-bomb casualties. He knew what had happened at Miyajima during the storm and kept asking how we had fared. The interpreter, I discovered, knew little Japanese, so what we had to communicate to each other was poorly relayed. After we had looked around and were making our way to the entrance, we ran into my wife. The officer asked if she had been injured and I told him she was anaemic and had received some wounds. I rolled up her sleeves and showed some scars. He nodded slightly and left.

After he had gone my heart pounded violently and my legs began to ache. I had forgotten to go down to the entrance with him, I was

48

so disturbed.[14]

Ten days later, two more groups of Americans visited the hospital. The first group 'made a minute examination of everything I called to their attention.' The second group in Dr Hachiya's account:

> ... had a Japanese-American interpreter whose family had come from Tanna. With this group I stayed in the improvised drawing-room and talked through the interpreter. One of the men stood at the window, looking over the ruins and, at length, said through the interpreter: 'There must be dead still in the ruins, and I have the feeling that if the ruins aren't removed and the bodies disposed of, ill-will between both countries will be prolonged. What is your opinion?'
>
> 'I agree with you,' I answered. 'I hear that you are using a useful machine in Kure to clear up the ruins, a "bulldozer" I think it is called. Couldn't you have one sent to help us clear up the city? Otherwise I am sure that those who were injured and those who lost relatives and friends will be continually reminded of the day they were bombed and hate you when you come back to Hiroshima.'
>
> 'It's out of the question,' the officer replied. 'America can't afford to send such equipment in here now. What are your thoughts about the bombing?'
>
> 'I am a Buddhist,' I replied, 'and since childhood have been taught to be resigned in the face of adversity. I have lost my home and my wealth, and I was wounded, but disregarding this, I consider it fortunate my wife and I are alive. I am grateful for this even though someone was to die in every home in my neighbourhood.'
>
> 'I can't share your feelings,' the officer replied sternly. 'If I were you, I'd sue the country.'
>
> The officer stood a while longer and gazed out the window. Finally, he and his party departed. After he had gone I told my friends what he said. 'Sue the country! Sue the country!' I repeated over and over to myself. But no matter how many times I repeated it, and however hard I thought, the statement was altogether incomprehensible.[15]

It was 'incomprehensible' unless one accepted the official American thesis that it was the Japanese leadership, the Emperor in particular, that was responsible for the A-bombing of

Hiroshima—not the United States. Dr Hichaya's diary ends at that point. By 30 September, twenty-seven days after the surrender had been signed, no American doctors had visited the Communications Hospital, or if there were any among the two groups mentioned, none had offered any advice as to how the survivors should be treated. In a postscript to his diary, Dr Hichaya notes that 'towards the middle of October, I was visited by Professor Sasa of Tokyo University, who brought an investigating committee of Americans. This group remained in Hiroshima for about a month, studying radiation sickness.' But there is no mention of any treatment or advice on treatment for the hospital inmates.

There is a fascinating earlier entry in Dr Hichaya's diary (15 August) which reflects the prestige and authority of the Emperor, unimaginable unless one has been in Japan. It is a phenomenon that everyone, left, right or centre in the political spectrum, has to take into account and which bears directly on the Japanese reactions to Hiroshima and Nagasaki.

> Word came to assemble in the office of the Communications Bureau. A radio had been set up and when I arrived the room was already crowded . ... In a few minutes, the radio began to hum and crackle with noisy static. One could hear an indistinct voice which only now and then came through clearly. I caught only one phrase which sounded something like, 'Bear the unbearable.' The static ceased and the broadcast was at an end.
>
> Chief Okamoto, who had been standing by the radio, turned to us and said: 'The broadcast was in the Emperor's own voice, and he has just said that we've lost the war. Until further notice, I want you to go about your duties.'
>
> I had been prepared for the broadcast to tell us to dig in and fight to the end, but this unexpected message left me stunned. It had been the Emperor's voice and he had read the Imperial Proclamation of Surrender. My psychic apparatus stopped working, and my tear glands stopped too. Like others in the room, I had come to attention at the mention of the Emperor's voice, and for a while we all remained silent and at attention. Darkness clouded my eyes, my teeth chattered, and I felt cold sweat running down my back.
>
> To myself I began denouncing the army: 'What do you fellows think about the Emperor? You started the war at your pleasure.

When the outlook was good, you behaved with importance, but when you began to lose, you tried to conceal your losses, and when you could move no more, you turned to the Emperor! Can you people call yourself soldiers? You have no choice but to commit *harakiri* and die!'

As if echoing my thoughts, someone shouted: 'General Tojo you great, thick-headed fool, cut your stomach and die!'[16]

Tojo intended to do just that, but lost his nerve at the last moment and tried to commit suicide with a pistol. I was in his room with other journalists seconds after he tried to put a bullet in his heart. We had accompanied US military police who were to arrest him at his Tokyo home, but were assured by the servant who answered the door bell that he had 'gone for a walk' and would soon be back. While the MPs were discussing what to do next, a shot rang out. When we rushed in, Tojo had collapsed into an arm-chair, feathers from a cushion behind his back floating down. On a table in front of him were laid out his sabre and *samurai* dagger, customarily used for a ritual *harakiri*. American medical personnel hastened to give a plasma transfusion; agency journalists fought each other to get to the telephone. Doctors succeeded in saving his life, temporarily. He lived to be tried as a war criminal and was hanged in December 1948.

I had sensed the contempt of troops towards the officer caste on my way to Hiroshima. But the feelings of civilians towards the military as a whole were expressed far more strongly during the return trip. In fact this was quite dramatic. Civilians who tried to board the train between Tokyo and Kyoto were roughly pushed back by the troops. On the return journey it was the civilians who just as roughly pushed back the troops, especially officers, who tried to board the train. This made a deep impression on me at the time, and on numerous subsequent visits I found that the strong anti-militarist feelings of the Japanese people had not subsided and there was widespread contempt for anyone in military uniform. But the Emperor remained sacrosanct.

Another extreme example of the heights or depths—according to how one views such matters—of Emperor worship is contained in Dr Hichaya's diary entry of 13 September, in which he relates how the Emperor's portrait was moved to a safe place while Hiroshima was an inferno of swirling flames, crammed with dead and dying—a city-sized crematorium. The occasion of the belated account was his meeting on that day a Mr Yasuda, 'who had the grave responsibility' for protecting the picture of the Emperor which hung in the city hall.

He was on a streetcar which had just reached Hakushima when the bomb exploded. Making his way through the darkened streets and around fallen houses, he managed to reach the Bureau ahead of the fires. His first act on arriving was to run to the fourth floor where the Emperor's picture hung and pry open an iron door behind which it was kept. With the assistance of Awaya, Oishi and Kagehira, he carried it to the chief's office and discussed with Mr Ushio what should be done with it. After much discussion it was decided the safest place would be the Hiroshima Castle, where less smoke appeared to be rising than elsewhere.

Thereupon the picture was placed on Mr Yasuda's back and with Mr Kagehira in the lead, Mr Ushio guarding the rear and Mr Awaya and Mr Oishi covering the flanks, they made their way to the inner garden of the Bureau and announced they were going to take the Emperor's picture to a safer place. Two or three times they repeated: 'The Emperor's picture will be transferred to the West Drill Field by the Chief of General Affairs!' Those among the staff and patients who heard this announcement bowed low and the procession went out through the back gate.

During its flight, the party encountered many dead and wounded, as well as soldiers near the barracks, the numbers increasing as they neared the dikes. Along the streetcar line circling the western border of the park they found so many dead and wounded they could hardly walk. At one point it became impossible, so great were the masses of people around them. The party shouted: 'The Emperor's picture! The Emperor's picture!' Those soldiers and citizens who could stood and saluted or bowed. Those who could not offered a prayer with hands clasped. Miraculously, the crowd opened and the picture was borne triumphantly to the river's edge!

'Oh, it was magnificent!', Mr Yasuda exclaimed. 'I gave the Emperor's picture to Chief Ushio and the chief got a boat someone unaccountably provided. An officer drew his sword and gave orders in a loud voice for the crossing and in response all the officers and soldiers lining the river bank stood at attention and saluted. Civilians stood in line and bowed. I can't explain how I felt, but I prayed that nothing would happen to the Emperor's picture ... Well, the river was calm and I can still picture Mr Ushio holding the Emperor's picture among the wounded soldiers.'

I might conclude Mr Yasuda's story by saying that shortly after Mr Ushio got the Emperor's picture safely across the river, the entire Futuba-no-Sato [city district] became a sea of fire. Whirlwinds and rain came. The river became turbulent and treacherous, its surface churned into great waves. Balls of fire flew over the river from the Futuba-no-Sato area and set fire to pine trees in Asano Sentei Park. As these great trees burned, swayed and toppled, the heat became unbearable. Houses were consumed and people crowding the river banks in an effort to escape the inferno, jumped in the river. Thousands were drowned. Mr Yasuda and Mr Oishi clung to a rock and escaped death.[17]

So much for Dr Tachiya's dramatic and often chilling account of what he and other Hiroshima survivors lived through during and immediately after the A-bomb holocaust. It requires no comment. My own last report from Japan was on the attempted suicide of General Tojo, following which I made a leisurely journey to London, via the United States, for reassignment.

4

Hiroshima: a Generation Later

During the first five post-war years, I covered the emerging 'Cold War' in Germany, and, when I could no longer tolerate that, I moved from Berlin to Budapest to report on the profound socio-economic and political transformations occuring in Eastern Europe. Still, Hiroshima's pulverized image continued to haunt me as each intensification of the Cold War revived the possibility of another nuclear holocaust. It could have happened in Germany at the turn of 1948/49 when the United States still basked in the certitude that it had the monopoly of nuclear weapons for many years to come. It could more easily have happened in Korea where the outbreak of a civil war in June 1950 was quickly transformed by Truman into an international conflict. Although the Soviet Union, contrary to all predictions, had already exploded its first A-bomb, the Truman administration was confident that with its huge bomber fleet and forward airbases, it retained a monopoly of means of 'delivery on target'.

When the Korean War broke out I was in Budapest as a stringer for *The Times* of London, having severed my relations with the *Daily Express* some months earlier. I received a cabled invitation from the Australian Peace Council to attend an inaugural conference in support of the Stockholm Appeal to ban the testing and production of nuclear weapons. I was to replace Paul Robeson as the keynote speaker after he was banned from travel abroad by the US government. I was at the summit of my career. Arthur Deakin, foreign editor of *The Times* had just offered me a staff correspondent's job whenever I wanted it. But the spectre of Hiroshima weighed heavily on my decision. Despite *The Times'* impeccable treatment of my reports, I had no hesitation in saying goodbye to Fleet Street and accepting the invitation from Australia. This was a watershed in my professional career and in my political options. I had become an aggressive peacenik!

Although I was treated with deference by the press on my arrival in my native Melbourne,—referred to as one of Australia's 'most distinguished journalists'—the tone soon changed. The rally to inaugurate the Stockholm Appeal was to have been held in the Melbourne Town Hall, especially booked for the occasion. Permission to use it was withdrawn at the last moment so the meeting took place on the Yarra Bank. (The Yarra is a small river which flows through Melbourne, the bank of which is traditionally a forum for free speech, a modest counterpart to London's Hyde Park or the Sydney Domain.) I quickly discovered that speaking against nuclear weapons in the Australia of Prime Minister Robert Gordon Menzies was just one step short of a crime. The Yarra Bank meeting went off well and—if I remember correctly—I had the honour of being the first signatory in the Australian campaign to 'Ban The Bomb'. I accompanied a delegation next morning to see Hubert Opperman, an international cycling champion, who was the mayor of Melbourne. Our purpose was to get another booking for the city hall.

'But I'm in charge of the recruiting committee for Korea,' replied Mayor Opperman. 'How can I let you have the city hall when you're talking about peace and banning nuclear weapons?' This set the pattern for the following four months, during which I spoke to audiences all over Australia, telling what I had seen in Hiroshima, while activists from local peace committees filled up endless pages with signatures backing the Stockholm Appeal. It was something like Henry Keys's battle with the US censors in Tokyo. Town halls, in big cities and down to the smallest parishes, would be hired, the fees pocketed by the authorities, and a few hours before a meeting—when it was too late to make other arrangements—permission to speak would be withdrawn. We countered by holding the meeting on the town hall steps, with the audience packed in around the steps and overflowing on to the footpaths. The police would come and charge us with 'obstructing traffic'.

The crowds were always large in proportion to the population of the localities. Interest in the subject was high and audiences listened with breathless interest to my accounts of what I had experienced in Hiroshima. The press, on the other hand, dropped me like a hot potato from the moment of the Yarra Bank rally when I announced for the first time that I had decided to quit Fleet Street journalism as long as the Cold War continued. Despite the participation of several distinguished public figures, the Yarra Bank meeting went unreported, as did the subsequent attempts to deny the peace movement a platform. Just as today, 'free speech' in the Australian daily press was carefully regulated by a handful of conservative newspaper barons.

Finally, we beat the 'obstructing traffic' charge by my walking backwards around the block on which the hall had been hired, guided by brawny arms, facing my audience who followed me round until the meeting, question time and all, was over. In between the evening public meetings were those at 'factory gates' at midday, unnerving until one gets used to it. The factory managers would not allow speakers inside, so at luncheon time you started speaking to locked gates. A few workers would come and unwrap their sandwiches and, if you had something interesting to say, a big crowd quickly collected. Questions were always to the point but time was obviously limited. Although there was a total blackout in the press—the Korean War got all the headlines with some of the most disgusting and callous reporting I have ever seen—there were always a few right-wingers in the audiences briefed to discredit what I had to say. A standard retort after I had described the horrors of Hiroshima was: 'So that's what the Russkies are preparing for us!' There would be some well-organized applause at this. The reply was easy: 'The Stockholm Appeal is for the banning of all nuclear weapons, whoever makes them. The difference between the Russian and Western official positions is that the Soviet Union strongly supports the Appeal whereas it is a "dirty word" for governments like ours.' A few jeers drowned by cheers. This was not a propaganda point but a reality which the

Australian people, like those of many other western countries, could never learn from their 'free press'.

It was a wearying four months but worthwhile and not without its unexpected moments. At a big steel works at Wollongong—forty miles south of Sydney—I spoke at a moderate-sized factory gate meeting on my way from Melbourne to the northern coastal areas. To my surprise I was asked to speak there again on my return journey. One of the organizers met me and exclaimed: 'Gee whizz, mate, you made a big hit last time. The men have been talking about it ever since. There's one bloke here who's never been in anything before—barely pays his union dues. But he's filled in more appeal forms than anyone. Know what his line is? He shoves the form with his pen ready under someone's nose. "Hey mate. Sign this," he says. "Hear what the Yanks did to the fish in Hiroshima?" Fishing's his only joy in life. You really got him in with that argument with the Yank general about the fish. Everyone's so happy to see him in something that they queued up to sign his forms.' It confirmed something I learned from my first public speech. You never know who you've touched and for what reason; sometimes not until many years later.

The 'Ban The Bomb' movement got off to a good start in Australia despite official obstruction and the press boycott of the Peace Council's activities. From that time onwards, successive right-wing Australian Governments (in power all but two years out of thirty-two) have had to take increasing account of the stubborn anti-nuclear stand of the vast majority of the Australian people. For example, Canberra has reluctantly had to champion the plea for a nuclear-free zone in the South Pacific and other anti-nuclear measures. The trade unions have carried out a major campaign against the mining and export of the country's rich reserves of uranium. Sydney was declared a nuclear-free city and adopted Hiroshima as its twin, and Melbourne was also declared nuclear-free, banning any entry of nuclear-armed or nuclear-powered vessels into its waters. The conservative Federal Government would not ratify these measures and, at the time of writing, it is a question as to whether or not the Labour Government, headed by Prime Minister Bob Hawke, voted into power in March 1983, will accede to the popular demand and ratify the status of Australia's two largest cities and support the trade unions in their stand against the mining and export of uranium ore.

After twenty years of reporting the wars in Korea and Indo-China, I finally returned to Hiroshima in 1971. I was delighted to find Dr Katsube still alive and active. He came to Hiroshima especially to meet me from the small island of Oki Gun in the Sea of Japan, where he was—and still is at the time of writing—running a tiny hospital with his wife for A-bomb survivors. I asked him what his thoughts were at the time of my visit and how the patients had reacted. He replied:

> We met for only a few hours. I asked your name and you replied, but I didn't catch it. I learned your name only many years later when I learned what you had written about your visit. One thing I felt was the difference between the rags we were wearing and you, well-dressed like a gentleman. The atmosphere was very tense and I was afraid for you.
>
> You were the first foreigner to come and we didn't know how to receive you. It was natural that the victims and their families felt hatred towards you. That's why I asked you to leave. I didn't want to risk the slightest incident. When we talked about it later, we felt you had come to do something about our plight. But didn't you feel afraid?

I explained that my feelings of horror at what had happened far outweighed any other emotions. My concern was to learn as much as possible as quickly as possible and inform the outside world. I asked whether he had suffered any ill-effects. He replied:

> No. I was outside the city when the bomb exploded and although I continued to work in the Communications Hospital until 1948, I have been lucky enough to escape the after-effects. I was struck, incidentally, that you were not armed. Of course, I thought you were an American. In fact, the Americans came much later—when the worst was over. Our impression was that they came more to observe and examine the results of our work, the progress of radiation sickness, than to help us, especially in the terrible situation during the first months.

This latter point was stressed in a meeting with editorial staff at

Chūgoku Press which produces the main Hiroshima daily newspaper. Staff members referred with sarcasm and bitterness to the Atomic Bomb Casualty Commission (ABCC) which President Truman ordered be set up at the end of November 1946. It commenced operation the following March in a grim, barracks-like building on a hill overlooking Hiroshima. The Chūgoku staff were unanimous that this was a research and not a treatment centre. Its findings were neither published nor made available to Japanese medical scientists. One of the editors said:

> The US personnel who work there have the status of diplomats. They were reputed to be very famous for their research skills but this did not lead to any treatment, or advice on treatment. Citizens of Hiroshima are indignant and feel they were treated like guineapigs—just models for theoretical experiments. We now believe that at the time the Americans dropped the A-bomb, the scientists who worked on it knew nothing about radiation nor how it effects people. They set up the ABCC to try to find out—for the protection of Americans in case they get involved in nuclear war. Usually such tests are first made on animals. We firmly believe that our people were selected to become the first test ground for the effects of A-bombs on human beings.
>
> By 1960, the American scientists had apparently achieved the main results of their research and so they released some of the results. But it was only after 1960 that Japanese scientists had access to some of these and could translate and publish them. Now the ABCC scientists have switched to another phase in their research—they are dealing with the genetic effects and studying the life cycle of the victims. We think that these activities are related to a possible World War III and the wholesale use of nuclear weapons.

Documents setting forth the framework in which the ABCC operated make it clear that it was purely a research organization. Thus Dr Stanley Finch, Chief of Medicine at the ABCC Hiroshima Centre from 1960-62, writes: 'The Atomic Bomb Casualty Commission began its work in Japan in 1947. Funded by the US Atomic Energy Commission, it was under the direction of the National Academy of Sciences National Research Council, for the purpose of long-term study of late radiation effects in both cities. The

Japanese National Institute of Health formally joined the studies in 1948. ... This successful bi-national research project is unique in the history of international human research, and is a testimony to the recognized importance of understanding of late radiation effects in man.'[18]

Ironically enough, all this elaborate research set-up was because of scientific acceptance of what the heads of the Manhattan Project, Generals Groves and Farrell, and their chief public relations adviser, W.L. Laurence, had so vehemently denied in the aftermath of the bombing. What many Japanese scientists and doctors can not forgive is that not only did these top-level American experts contribute nothing to alleviate the sufferings of the survivors, but they did not communicate their findings to their Japanese counterparts in good time either. This, together with the ban on independent Japanese research which had treatment as its main priority, blocked for many years any scientifically-based treatment of the victims.

There are gruesome stories told in Hiroshima about the activities of the ABCC which one could write off as propaganda, if they were not confirmed by American documentation. Special teams tracked down survivors, even if they had settled elsewhere, and all sorts of pressures short of brute force were used to get them behind the doors of the ABCC centre. Like the warning posted over the entrance to Dante's *Inferno*, it was a case of 'Leave Every Hope Behind You Who Enter Here'. Those selected as in-patients never came out. Nor could relatives visit them. Dr Finch admitted this implicitly when he wrote: 'The base population for the Pathology Study consists of a sub-set of persons in the Life-Span Study, who reside in the Hiroshima-Nagasaki area and are candidates for post-mortem studies at the time of death. Autopsy rates as high as 45 per cent in the early 1960s have provided information of great value in confirmation of death certificate diagnoses and the histological description of radiation-induced tumours....'[19]

This is ghoulish language. I didn't publish what I was told in Hiroshima in 1971 because I had no way of confirming the statements and suppositions of those with whom I spoke. Finch's observations were published only ten years later. 'Candidates for post-mortem studies' among a 'sub-set of persons' conjures up the vision of professional body-snatchers—but snatching while the bodies were still alive—with a sure and legal market for their stock in trade. The ABCC had an insatiable appetite for 'post-mortem' candidates while they were still warm. Indeed, the bulk of the American scientists and medical experts who came to Hiroshima in those early years were infinitely more interested in the dead and dying than they were in those who could be helped to survive.[20]

The *Hibakusha*

Among the unscheduled events during my 1971 visit to Hiroshima was a welcoming ceremony at the Atomic Bomb Commemoration Hall. It was presided over by Mayor Takeshi Araki, who presented me with a bronze plaque for my contribution to the anti-nuclear movement. In an impromptu speech thanking the Mayor, I recalled my emotions during my 1945 visit and commented that the world-wide revulsion against what had happened had stayed the hands of the nuclear war zealots ever since. Perhaps this was some slight comfort for the survivors and relatives of the victims of the world's greatest man-made catastrophe. I noted that Hiroshima had been beautifully rebuilt, with spacious parks and gardens replacing the ghastly devastated spaces I had seen during my first visit. It had also become a rallying point for those who sought and fought for peace, but enough of the horrors had been preserved in parks and museums to remind people of that terrible day of 6 August 1945.

It was not much of a speech, the best I could do on the spur of the moment. Despite some polite applause, I felt that I had not really touched my audience, something which every public speaker is sensitive to. Next morning, I was informed that a group of young people were waiting in the hotel lobby to see me. They were from a recently-formed organization called HISEIDO (acronym for Hibakusha[21] Seinen Domei) or Youth League of A-bomb Victims. After enquiring politely as to whether a meeting was convenient, a young woman, Miss Hasegawa, came forward as spokesperson. She was twenty-six—born in the Year of the Bomb...

'My impression of listening to your speech last night,' she said, 'is that you have only superficially grasped what is really happening here. The victims are pushed into the background, at the bottom of the social strata. We feel that as you came to speak in Hiroshima, you should have delved far more deeply into the social condition of the *hibakusha*.' This was the first time I had heard the term. In fact I was in Japan at the invitation of some anti-war groups to generate support for Vietnam. I had no idea I was to speak about Hiroshima until a few seconds before I was on my feet. I explained this, adding that it would have been better had the group come to see me before I spoke. But Miss Hasegawa continued imperturbably.

'Nevertheless, before speaking on such an important theme, we think you should have informed yourself better. However, some of the things you said are the key to questions which bother our people. You spoke of the Appeal to the People of Hiroshima for no more nuclear wars having aroused the conscience of the world. Such things are used to oppress and silence us, the victims. Immediately after the surrender, restrictions were put on the press. This meant that just those who most urgently needed to raise their voices could not do so. If they did, they just disappeared. Many preferred to pay that price and did speak out. But who could hear them when the press and radio were gagged?'

To my question as to what they wanted to say, she replied passionately: 'The victims, of whom our group is part, still live under the shadow of the A-bomb. We, children of the second generation, live under constant fear that our health will deteriorate. You spoke of the beautiful parks and gardens. Yes, they are beautiful and they have beautifully covered up the ruins but they cannot cover up what may be inside all the survivors. A study has been carried out at Yamaguchi University on children of the first generation victims. [It turned out that Ms Hasegawa was a medical student at that university.] This showed that one in four suffers from defects. One child, born twenty years after the Bomb, had similar symptoms to those of the original victims and died.' She explained that the symptoms were chronic weakness and periods of extreme lassitude, sufficient to discourage any employer from hiring a *hibakusha*.

I had heard that the Emperor and Empress had visited Hiroshima a few months earlier. Did this not mean that the authorities were going to pay more attention to the Hiroshima survivors? 'Exactly the contrary', exclaimed Ms Hasegawa. Everybody then wanted to speak at once. A young man explained that anything which the Emperor said or did in Japan had great significance, not always apparent on the surface. 'Even "we of the left" have to admit that his authority is enormous. In the twenty-six years since the Bomb, the Emperor had never before come to Hiroshima. Nor had any prime minister come to see for himself.' The interpretation of Ms Hasegawa's group was that by his visit he wanted to please the Americans by saying, in effect: Now all is over. Let's forget and forgive about the Bomb and the sufferings!

'And in his style this is what he did,' she continued. 'But we don't accept this and the people of Hiroshima don't accept it. If you got a cool reception last night to some of the things you said, it is because many of those present suspected you were peddling the "forget and forgive" nonsense. Now Prime Minister Eisaku Sato is to come. We are trying to stop this. The press reported that the Hiroshima victims were happy about the Emperor's visit and would be happy with Sato's visit. In fact,' she said, ignoring the horrified looks of Japanese hotel guests who had gathered around to listen, 'we would kill Sato if we could.' I recognized among the attentive listeners one—certainly from one of Japan's numerous security services—who had assiduously followed me from the time of my arrival at Tokyo's Haneda airport. He was finally getting full value for his tenacity!

'We hate Sato,' continued Ms Hasegawa. 'You must understand why we feel so bitter against him. He does only what the Americans want him to do. When the Emperor came the city was cleaned up—which meant the victims were pushed still further into the background. The Emperor did not visit the A-bomb hospital or the Exhibition. We criticize the Exhibition because what it shows is far from the reality of what happened. But he didn't visit even that. He was taken to see some victims and murmured:

"Please get well soon!" In fact they were all incurable cases!

'You came out of last night's meeting with garlands of peace cranes round your neck.'

These are paper cut-outs to symbolize peace and long life. They decorate all the memorial figures and statues in Hiroshima. The idea was launched there—each 'crane' representing a prayer for peace from the little girls who make them.

'They are perhaps beautiful symbols, but out of place in Hiroshima. The American Iwakuni Air Base is only a few miles away and is being expanded every day. Is that peace? The garlands are part of the cover-up of the real situation here.'

I asked if there were any reliable figures on what she referred to as second-generation victims?

'There has been no proper survey of second generation victims so far,' she replied. 'Whether they run into tens of thousands or hundreds of thousands, we cannot know. Many parents hide the symptoms in their children for fear of future discrimination.... Victims and their descendants are spread all over Japan—many fled the city because they could not live with such a nightmare.

'A woman writer, Shoda Shinda, who wrote a book of poems about Hiroshima and had to circulate it secretly because of the US press laws, later died of radiation sickness. Another writer and poet, Togo Sankichi, did his best to appeal to people and wake them up as to what was going on. But how to reach the public? Many creative intellectuals died of the sickness, others committed suicide. People who come from outside to work in Hiroshima, have a slogan: "Don't marry a Hiroshima girl" because they fear for the after-effects. Such words wounded us deeply at first—but I myself, after the studies at Yamaguchi University, fear to have a child in case it should be malformed.

'Many doctors feel that radiation effects will come out more strongly still in the third generation. And that even their children will carry the mysterious X to be inherited. It is too early to know for sure. Twenty five is the greatest age of those conceived since the A-bomb, so there is not enough statistical evidence to make a judgement. I know a number of young people who have married and have children that so far seem healthy. But others with defects are not identified, either by their parents or by the public health authorities. This is proof that neither the Government nor the Municipality have made scientific studies. Among other factors, they are scared of the extra financial burden if they have to look after the *hibakusha.*'

As to how many of the Hiroshima survivors could be considered as still affected, Ms Hasekawa replied: 'Psychologically all are affected. There is the fear of what may come tomorrow, what may happen to their children and their children's children. There are many people who have lost almost all capacity to exert themselves —the bosses and authorities put this down to chronic laziness and there is no data to prove the contrary. But we know that these are simply, unclassified, unrecognized victims of radiation.

'According to the Radiation Medical Sickness Law, the Government must carry out surveys and recognize instances of radiation sickness. Only 6,000 so far have been recognized and of these, only 1,000 from Hiroshima. These get free medical treatment. Many don't want to register for fear of discrimination in getting jobs or in finding a marriage partner. But many who do want to register cannot because of the unfair and arbitrary stands for "recognition" set by the Government because of the financial costs involved.'

I asked if the ABCC had not worked out some fool-proof criteria by which radiation sickness and genetic effects could be established?

'The ABCC brought in their best US genetic experts, with completed and up-to-date files on the survivors. They have made very careful surveys, going to homes and factories, even schools, to put such pressures on the victims that they could hardly refuse to cooperate. If a known victim dies, they make sure that they get their hands on the body. But the findings are not published and we think the victims are used as guinea-pigs for military research....'

It had been a most illuminating hour and caused me to deviate from my day's programme. At the Red Cross and Atom Bomb Victims' Hospital, I asked the director, Dr Shigetö, whether Ms Hasegawa's charges were well-founded. 'Absolutely,' he replied, 'but it is difficult to prove anything. For instance, if we take leukemia (blood cancer) cases, normally these occur in two to three per 100,000 of the population; in Hiroshima, the rate for those within one kilometre of the epicentre is 125 per 100,000; for those up to one and a half kilometres it is 25; and for those up to two kilometres, 5 per 100,000. The inference is clear, but which of those 125, 25 or 5 per hundred thousand cases is due to atomic radiation, no one can prove—at least not with present techniques. Other types of cancer of which the incidence is high are those of the thyroid, breast and stomach. The incidence curve of all these—plus liver disturbances, pernicious anaemia, lymphocemia and others—grows higher also in proportion to the victim's closeness to the epicentre. But we still have no way of discerning which cases are the direct result of the radiation diffused by the A-bomb.'

'As for the psychological effect, this is very great.' He took me to see one of his in-patients, a Mrs Onoyo Yamamoto who had lost four children in the original blast. She spoke of a son who was one-year-old at the time and survived. 'He's getting on alright so far,' she said, 'and was engaged to be married. But after I was admitted to hospital six years ago the girl's family forced her to break the betrothal. They fear that whatever I have got will be transmitted through him. So he can't marry for fear of the future.' She started sobbing and the doctor led me away.

'Nobody knows how many thousands of such cases there are,' he said. 'Mrs Yamamoto even has a guilt complex that she is responsible for her son's wrecked life. The only way we can keep such patients with hypoprastic anaemia alive is through regular blood transfusions.' I asked Dr Shigetö if he had any cases of children born of a mother pregnant at the time of the explosion? 'There are plenty on our out-patients list,' he replied and gave my guide a few names and addresses. One of these brought us to a Mr Hatanake, a barber at Iwakuni, about twenty miles southwest of Hiroshima. A small, lively man with a plumpish wife, they had a dull-eyed daughter who sat with her head bowed, fingering a picture magazine during our visit. His wife, Yurika (Lily) was diffident about relating her experiences so it was Hatanake-*san* who did the talking:

'I was in the Army so not at home at the time of the *pikadon*',[22] he said. 'Each family had to send one member to clear breaks in case Hiroshima was fire-bombed as Tokyo had been. Yurika went that day with our one-year-old child on her back. She was sent to a spot about 700 metres from where the bomb exploded. Because she had a baby on her back and was also pregnant, the other women decided she should not do hard work and assigned her to look after the luncheon boxes. She was stacking these up inside an above-ground concrete shelter, about the size of a telephone booth, when the flash occurred. All the others were killed immediately, but she only blacked out. When she came to all she could see were ruins and fires. She started running instinctively towards the hills. By the time she got to the last patch of ricefields before the high ground, black rain started falling.'

Many survivors spoke of this phenomenon. It was not normal rain. Scientists later said that it was large drops of moisture formed by minute particles of carbon thrown up by the heat, forming water vapour when it reached layers of cold air. These became charged with radioactive dust and fell in isolated showers of what everyone referred to as 'black rain'.

'She found shelter in a shack with some other people and set about feeding the baby. His face was pitted with glass splinters, the biggest of which she removed. When the rain stopped she set out for the hills again, wandering about there, eating whatever she could find, then headed for our own house. Soon afterwards Yurika's hair started falling out, then she developed small boils and started bleeding from various parts of her body.

'By the time I was demobilized and returned home, Yurika was completely bald. The little boy started showing the same symptoms, but accompanied by diarrhoea. We managed to contact a doctor, but he knew nothing about radioactivity at that time. The baby was treated for dysentery but soon died. Afterwards the doctors believed that the baby on my wife's back acted as a shield, absorbing most of the deadly rays and thus saving her life.

'A girl baby was born on 14 February 1946, which means that my wife was about three months pregnant at the time of the Bomb. Her body and left leg were slightly crooked. Yurika massaged the leg all the time—and still does—trying to strengthen and stretch it. But she walked on all fours for longer than normal. We thought she was just retarded and would grow out of it in time. We had no money for medical treatment. Gradually she could stand up, but she was wobbly from the waist down. She has no control over urination or defecation. Although she has picked up some words from the TV, she can neither converse, nor read and write. Until five or six years ago, we thought our daughter was the only case of this kind. But in 1965, some friends started to investigate and soon found eighteen similar cases, one of whom died last year. A committee was set up and until now has found forty-five such young people in Hiroshima similarly affected.

'I am fighting', continued barber Hatanake, 'to have her case recognized for several reasons. The Government should "recognize" her so that she can have continual medical care. We want her to be assured of institutional care when we die. And we think that there must be some useful therapy for cases like hers. My wife's capacity for this is limited. Not only due to lack of knowledge, but she suffers from anaemia and has dizzy and fainting spells. After all she has been through, it is not surprising that she also suffers from chronic depression.'

Before leaving Hiroshima on that memorable first return trip, I saw Dr Shigetö again and he confirmed that Mr Hatanake's account was correct and corresponded to what had happened to other cases that had been brought to the hospital's attention.

Following subsequent visits to Hiroshima (especially those in 1981 and 1982) and having read much in the meantime, I wrote to Dr Katsube for a more precise account of his activities in the months which immediately followed the dropping of the Bomb. Also I asked what proportion of those patients whom I had seen had survived? His reply is dated 24 October 1982 and reads in part as follows:

> The day when Mr Burchett visited the Hiroshima Communications Hospital was 3 September 1945. On that day, doctors of hospitals in Hiroshima, as well as an investigating team centering around Professor Tzuzuki of Tokyo University, had gathered and were discussing the atomic bomb disease.... The victims you ask about are not in this hospital now. An American military doctors'

group who came later were enthusiastically investigating radiation sickness and asking questions. They seemed to be studying very carefully, meticulously checking our research record.

Regarding your questions... dealing with symptoms and treatment, to observe the processes of the sufferers after the Bomb, I have divided these into three periods: first period, 6 August to 19 August; second period, 20 August to 15 September; and third period, 16 September to end of October.

Many sufferers hospitalized during the *first period* were within 1,000 metres of the epicentre, almost all of whom were affected with: small hypodermal bleeding (almost the whole body); dysentery-type entero-hemorrhage, haematuria, bleeding of genitals, and so on; and bleeding from the nose which could not be stopped. Almost all died after a couple of days of suffering. There were about 150 people who took refuge in the Hiroshima Communications Hospital during the first period, of whom about 50 per cent are presumed to have died. Those who survived were people who were better protected, such as under a concrete building.

Atomic bomb sufferers during the *second period* were in the area from 1,000 to 1,500 metres from the epicenter. This spans the period when you came on 3 September. By this time sufferers were having hypodermal bleeding, internal bleeding, as well as *datsuryokukan* (total enervation), languor of the whole body, vomiting, *alopecia* (depilatory disease), etc. The colour of the skin and face of patients became brown (liver colour) or bluish white. To investigate the cause of this disease, I did post-mortem autopsy on 26 August for the first time, and found a lot of bleeding in internal organs, chest and abdomen. It was presumed that the occurrence of sudden death was caused by heart bleeding. I carried out nine further autopsies after that.

Mr Burchett came by car and went into the hospital alone where about seventy *hibaku* patients, with only the clothes on their back, were lying on thin spreads on the concrete floor and the place was so crowded that there was hardly space to walk. Watching Mr Burchett, who went inside among the *hibakusha* who were injured and fell ill because of the atomic bomb and sure to be burning with anger, I felt him to be a saint who does not fear.

When blood transfusions were done to counter the bleeding, patients felt a chill and trembled. Also chills came when intravenous injections, such as sugar, were given... When you visited the hospital, the rate of deaths of *hibaku* victims was probably more than 60 per cent. Almost all of these people, I think, had radiation sickness (*genbaku* disease) caused by radiation....

Dr Gen Katsube, as mentioned earlier, was essentially a surgeon and his essay, 'On the Cause of Scar and Keloid of A-Bomb Exposed People' is considered the most authoritative work on the subject. In none of our discussions, did he deal with the psychological consequences of the Bomb.

The Survivors Fight Back

In the excellently documented Japanese book on Hiroshima and Nagasaki referred to earlier, a whole chapter is devoted to the psychological after-effects on the survivors. By the time the book was published, and due to great pressure on the government by medical scientists and *hibakusha* organizations, a survey had been made, revealing the astonishing figure of 370,000 survivors suffering from the effects of the Bomb. And, as the doctor in charge of the Hiroshima hospital for A-bomb victims told me, during another visit in May 1980, this figure was far from complete. 'In order to be recognized as a victim,' he explained, 'it is necessary to have two witnesses—relatives—willing to swear that the person concerned was in Hiroshima at the time of the explosion, or within the following two weeks. But many victims lost every family member at the time. As for the military who were there, they had no relatives to vouch for them.'

The official recognition that people were afflicted by radiation sickness who were not even in Hiroshima at the time the Bomb was detonated but who entered the city in the two weeks that followed, gave the lie to the Groves–Farrell–Laurence version and fully corroborated what I had reported in the *Daily Express* at the time. It also confirmed what I had long suspected, that the Americans were in such a hurry to test the bomb on live targets that they had not bothered to investigate the possible consequences.

Some extracts from the chapter on psychological trends bear out Ms Hasegawa's assertions that all the survivors were affected psychologically:

> The 370,000 A-bomb victims in Japan and the several thousands in other countries naturally have different personalities as well as, in some cases, different nationalities... That is not to say however, that they have nothing in common psychologically....Certainly the most sweeping and searing destruction ever visited upon mankind left an enormous, abhorrent and lifelong impression in the minds and memories of its victims. Even today, over thirty years after the bombings, there is no end to the hundreds of diaries, testimonies and drawings that annually come from the hands of the victims, some of which gain the attention of the mass media. Despite the passage of time, the memories of these survivors are strikingly vivid and concrete.... The startling lucidity of the A-Bomb victims' memories is surely one proof of the enormity of the psychological shock they suffered....

Based on investigations and analyses of thousands of survivors by some of Japan's most prestigious psychologists, the account continues with a description of the forms of lingering psychological suffering.

> The rebuilt lives of A-Bomb victims remained precarious for various reasons. First of all, there was always the threat to their health from delayed radiation effects. Second, there was the fear that their children would be unhealthy or deformed. Third, economic instability threatened if delayed radiation effects decreased their ability to work or care for themselves and also required increased medical expenses. Fourth, death, sickness and decline or loss of ability to work and manage could further accelerate the disintegration of victims' families. Fifth, discrimination against them by non-victims added to life's difficulties. These multiple effects on health, life and livelihood imposed a great psychological burden on A-bomb victims. Their efforts to rebuild were extremely vulnerable to setbacks from external factors, and not a few survivors saw their efforts collapse two, three, or more times...[23]

The authors go on to describe many variants of the few cases I had seen many years earlier and about which I have written. They were only too tragically similar. In another work, *A Call From Hibakusha of Hiroshima and Nagasaki*, which was the outcome of an International Symposium, held in the two stricken cities between 21 July and 9 August 1975, a sixth plight of the *hibakusha* was mentioned: the psychosis cased by the testing of ever more powerful nuclear weapons:

> Throughout these thirty-two years, the anguish of the *hibakusha* has not been lessened. Rather, it has been intensified by the increased arms race and the repeated A-bomb tests which make the *hibakusha* feel that their appeals have not been heard and their experience has been in vain. Their anguish has been increased by facts revealed by historical research into the decision to drop the bombs. The evidence seems to point to the conclusion that the use of atomic bombs was not necessary to bring an end to the war and, rejecting a number of other options, a decision was made to use the atomic bombs on cities whose population density was high. Thus, it seems to many *hibakusha* that the atomic bombings were big demonstrations aimed at influencing Soviet behaviour, and the *hibakusha* feel that far from being sacrifices for peace, they were merely objects whose suffering and death were without meaning.[24]

The citizens of Hiroshima and Nagasaki were—and this point cannot be emphasized too strongly—victims of deliberate medical experimentation and cold war political expediency. In my frequent visits to Japan since 1971, I have watched the process of national opinion gradually registering and absorbing the enormity of the cover-up involved, including the elaborate 'forgive and forget' campaign. If Japan has the largest and most vigorous peace movement in the world, it is partially because of the popular 'gut' reaction to the ceaseless official attempts to instil national amnesia and to deny the continuing tragedy of the *hibakusha*.

The psychological depression and isolation of the *hibakusha* has been relieved by publicity, and the fast-growing anti-nuclear movement has had a positive therapeutic effect. From outcasts hiding their wounds in shame, they got together and displayed their wounds and scars at home and abroad, using them as weapons in the campaign for a world without nuclear weapons. Who was better placed to be in the frontline of the struggle? This started with the formation of small groups of survivors who, after the shocking neglect of the first decade after the A-bomb was used against them, refused to accept the official concealment of their plight.

A major breakthrough came when the First World Conference Against A- and H-bombs was held in Hiroshima in August 1975. The Japanese people, not to mention the international participants, heard for the first time the horrors from the lips of those who had been the victims. Gradually over the years, their organization became more cohesive, and their demands increased from the modest request for some free medical treatment, to the demand for a national law providing indemnities for all survivors. By the mid 1970s the *hibakusha* had their own national organization, the *HIDYANKO*, Japanese Confederation of A- and H-bomb sufferers. (The latter could by then be included because of the incident which occurred when the United States tested its first H-bomb on the Bikini Atoll in the Marshall Islands, on 1, March 1954. Radioactive ashes fell on the Japanese fishing boat 'Lucky Dragon', 160 kilometres distant. One crewman later died, the other twenty-two were stricken with radiation sickness. The fish catch had to be destroyed and a vast area of traditional fishing grounds had to be abandoned. Radioactive ashes also fell on Japan itself.)

The numbers of the *hibakusha* remain shocking. As mentioned earlier, the government survey came up with a minimum of 366,523 survivors. Apart from the rigorous criteria adopted for the 'recognition' of Japanese survivors, which exluded large numbers, the figure also excludes an estimated 23,000 Korean victims who were expatriated immediately after the explosion. They had been brought to Japan to work with virtually slave status during the Japanese occupation of 'The Land of Morning Calm', as the Koreans call their beautiful country. The almost 370,000 'recognized' victims included 179,637 in Hiroshima, 109,936 in Nagasaki and 76,950 spread around 45 other prefectures—as of March 1977.

Encouraged by the successes of the pioneers of their movement, the *hibakusha* have rallied around their national movement which has now become a force to be reckoned with, by all political parties. They have their groups within the political parties and in the powerful trade-union movement. Their 'Health Notebooks' represent a guarantee that they can no longer be arbitrarily fired from their jobs for 'chronic laziness'. They have the support of all the opposition parties in the Diet (National Assembly) — a well-deserved award for their stubborn, up-hill struggle, and of the support the most progressive elements at all levels of Japanese society.

5

Was It All Necessary?

On 16 July 1945, Secretary of Defence, Henry L. Stimson slipped a note across the table to President Truman, then discussing post-war policies at Potsdam with Churchill and Stalin. The message said simply: 'It's a boy!' Truman understood that the A-bomb had been successfully tested at Alamogordo, New Mexico. Awaiting such a message with great impatience, he had even succeeded in delaying the start of the conference to ensure the right timing. Stimson notes that Truman had gone to Potsdam wanting and expecting Soviet intervention against Japan (as Stalin had previously guaranteed Roosevelt), but that with the message from Alamogordo his position 'hardened noticeably'. 'As sole possessor of the bomb, he had good reason to expect easier future dealings with Stalin.' He quotes Truman as confiding to one of his advisers: 'If it explodes, as I think it will, I'll certainly have a hammer on those boys (the Russians).'[25]

Churchill was also impressed by the sudden change of Truman's demeanour at the conference table. 'Truman was evidently much fortified by something that had happened and... he stood up to the Russians in a most emphatic and decisive manner.' After reading the full report on the Alamogordo explosion, Churchill said, 'Now I know what happened to Truman yesterday. I couldn't understand. When he got to the meeting after having read this report he was a changed man. He told the Russians just where they got off and generally bossed the whole meeting.' Churchill's Chief of Staff, Lord Alanbrooke, noted in his diary that his boss 'was completely carried away... we now had something in our hands which would redress the balance with the Russians. The secret of this explosive and the power to use it could completely alter the diplomatic equilibrium... Now we had a new value which redressed our position (pushing out his chin and scowling): now we could say: "If you insist on doing this or that well... And then where were the Russians?"'[26]

The diaries and memoirs of various Allied participants all agree that at Yalta six months earlier a major concern had been to extract a pledge from Stalin to enter the war against Japan within three months of victory over the Nazis, and that they came to Potsdam (Truman having succeeded Roosevelt by that time) with the same preoccupation: 'Would Stalin honour his pledge?' All this went by the board once the 'It's a boy' message was received. Churchill reported back to his Cabinet: 'It is quite clear that the United States do not at the present time desire Russian participation in the war against Japan.'[27]

It was assumed that Stalin had no idea that an A-bomb had been successfully tested, but he could scarcely avoid noticing the abrupt change in Truman's attitude. In his *Memoirs*, the Soviet Chief of Staff, Marshal Georgi Zhukov, described Stalin's reaction:

> The Conference finished work on 2 August. While it was still in session, the head of the US government, President Truman, with the aim of political blackmail, tried to carry out a psychological attack against J.V. Stalin. I don't recall the exact date, but after a meeting of the Heads of Governments, President Truman informed J.V. Stalin of the existence of bombs of unprecedented power, without naming them as A-bombs. At the time this information was conveyed—as was later written abroad—Churchill looked fixedly at Stalin's face to watch his reaction. But the latter in no way showed any particular feeling, as if there was nothing exceptional in what H. Truman had said. As the British and Americans have written, they concluded that Stalin had probably not grasped the significance of this information.
>
> In fact, on the way back from the meeting, Stalin in my presence told (foreign minister) V.M. Molotov of the conversation he had just had with Truman. Molotov remarked: 'He's trying to raise his price.' Stalin laughed: 'Let him raise it. We must speak again with Kurchatov and tell him to get a move on with our work.' I then

understood that it was a question of the A-bomb.[28]

It is thus quite clear from the Potsdam memoirs that the *hibakusha* were later correct in assuming that the atomic bombings were big demonstrations aimed at influencing Soviet behaviour. But what was Washington's initial impetus in diverting the giant resources involved in Project Manhattan? According to the official version, Roosevelt's original decision had been prompted by the urgent lobbying of eminent scientists—many of them, like Einstein or Fermi, refugees from fascism—who warned that the German breakthroughs in solving the theoretical problems of nuclear fission might soon be translated into the production of a monstrous weapon.

Later, these same scientists—always in contact with some of their former colleagues inside Germany — realized that the Nazis, sabotaged by some of their elite scientists and the crippling of industry by Allied bombings, were in fact incapable of building an A-bomb. Their reaction was to propose that the Americans halt their efforts. They were well-enough informed to be fearful of the long-term results of their handiwork and were mainly men of conscience. But the military Manhattan Project planners worked ever more feverishly to produce the Bomb, still insisting that it was a race against time. This was true, but the arguments used were false. General Groves and his team knew that Germany was out of the race to build a nuclear device, and that the United States would not only produce the first A-bomb, it would also have monopoly on nuclear weapons. The race against time was to be able to demonstrate this unprecedented power before the Nazis capitulated. In a filmed interview with Pathé Cinema shortly after his exploit, Lt. Col. Paul Tibbetts, the pilot of the *Enola Gay* (the plane that destroyed Hiroshima), revealed that two separate air crews were organized well before the first successful test of the Bomb. One was for bombing targets in Germany, the other for Japan in case the war in Europe ended before the Bomb was operational. He said he had no scruples about it because it would save American lives.

The Race That Humanity Lost

The period immediately following the First World War seemed a Golden Age for those scientists who, unwittingly at the time, were to become the godparents and midwives of nuclear weaponry. They probed subatomic Nature's most intimate secrets to find the means of releasing unfathomably powerful sources of energy. The way forward was first shown by the great New Zealand scientist, Ernest (later Lord) Rutherford, when he succeeded during the First World War in splitting the nitrogen atom after bombardment with alpha particles. Many of the world's most brilliant scientists converged in the twenties on one of the three great centres of atomic physics (later commuting between all three): Cambridge where Rutherford had a headstart; Copenhagen's University, where Niels Bohr, one of the most prestigious of Rutherford's contemporaries, headed the Physics Institute; and Göttingen where, in the halcyon days of the Weimar Republic, world-famous theorists like Max Born, James Franck, and David Hilbert dominated the faculty of physics at the Georgia Augusta University.

In the best scientific traditions, they were internationalists. The life-blood of progress depended on generous exchanges of information, especially the results of each other's research. For a certain period, the beautiful old city of Göttingen was the Mecca of the world's most outstanding physicists—and those seeking this elevated status. Among the latter was a young American student who came to listen and to learn in 1926. Apparently considered rather garrulous and boring by some of his elders, he was also recognized as something of a genius. Thus was J. Robert Oppenheimer initiated into the ranks of the latter-day alchemists of Göttingen, eventually earning the doubtful distinction of becoming known as the father of the A-bomb. Among others later to rank among the giants of nuclear physics, Leo Szilard and Edward Teller, found the Weimar Republic more conducive for study and experimentation than their native Hungary under the fascist regime of Admiral Horthy. Places for Jews, like themselves, were so restricted in Hungary's universities that it was impossible for them to pursue their research.

By the early 1930s, however, with the rise of Hitler, the chill wind of anti-semitism began to blow with ever-increasing force and even Göttingen was not spared. Within a month of Hitler's accession to power, the first blow fell when seven members of the Natural Sciences Faculty of the University, including Max Born, were summarily dismissed. James Franck, although also Jewish, was not on the list of those dismissed, presumably because of his great international reputation, but he resigned to show his solidarity. Thus started the process during which Nazi Germany 'blew out its brains'. Those who had previously fled to Germany from Poland and Hungary did not wait to be expelled or arrested, but left for Copenhagen, where they were welcomed with open arms and hearts by Niels Bohr and his colleagues.

The exiles, whether they ultimately ended up in Denmark, England or the United States, maintained precarious contacts with their old colleagues in Germany. Early in 1939 news filtered through to America that the greatest of the German scientists who still remained in the Third Reich had been mobilized for what was code-named the 'U-project' to research uranium fission. Shortly after these first reports, there came a sinister confirmation: Germany banned the export of uranium oxide from Czechoslovakia after occupying that country in May. Szilard, Teller and Fermi (who had fled from Italian fascism) were all in the United States by this time. They well understood the implications and were stupefied by the prospect of atomic power being harnessed to Hitler's war machine. However their first attempts to alert US military authorities to the potential menace were fruitless. Although their reputations were appreciated by American scientific contemporaries, they were without influence in military circles. In the military mind they were merely 'eggheads' or even 'crackpots'.

Eventually Szilard and Eugene Wigner, a German-born exile and long-time collaborator of Bohr, managed to get the ear of Albert Einstein, who, until the meeting, had previously disclaimed the feasibility of a large-scale atomic chain-reaction—an opinion also shared by Rutherford until his death. When Szilard and Wigner explained the potential in splitting the uranium atom,

Einstein grasped the point immediately and agreed to support them in persuading the US government to buy up Belgium's entire uranium stock (which originated from what was then the Belgian Congo). It was an urgent question of forestalling Hitler from grabbing the stocks himself when, as the military strategists all agreed, the German war machine would again follow the 'swinging door' through the Low Countries. Einstein added the prestige of his signature to a letter to President Roosevelt to this effect. But how to get the letter—plus a memorandum recommending that the United States should also explore the military potential of atomic power—into the hands of one of the world's busiest statesmen?

Through one of his contacts, Szilard was put in touch with Alexander Sachs, an international financier and scholar, highly respected by Roosevelt for his uncanny accuracy in analysing long-range economic trends and also for his absolute discretion. Sachs was won over to Szilard's ideas and agreed to deliver the letter and memorandum to Roosevelt personally. This he did on 11 October 1939. To heighten the effect, he read out both documents. The president was not very impressed, but sensing that Sachs attached great importance to the matter, invited him to breakfast the following morning. All night Sachs racked his brains as to how to plead more effectively a cause which he had become convinced was of crucial importance.

Robert Jungk describes what happened on the next morning:

> Roosevelt was sitting alone at the breakfast table in his wheel chair when Sachs entered the room. The President inquired in an ironical tone:
>
> 'What bright idea have you got now? How much time would you like to explain it?'
>
> Dr Sachs says he replied that he would not take long. 'All I want to do is to tell you a story. During the Napoleonic wars a young American inventor named Fulton came to the French Emperor and offered to build a fleet of steamships with the help of which Napolean could, in spite of the uncertain weather, land in England. Ships without sails? This seemed to the great Corsican so impossible that he sent Fulton away. The English historian Lord Acton used this as an example of how England was saved by the short-

sightedness of an adversary. Had Napoleon shown more imagination and humility at that time, the history of the nineteenth century would have taken a very different course.'

After Sachs finished speaking, the President remained silent for several minutes. Then he wrote something on a scrap of paper and handed it to the servant who had been waiting at the table. The latter soon returned with a parcel which, at Roosevelt's order, he began slowly to unwrap. It contained a bottle of old French brandy of Napoleon's time, which the Roosevelt family had possessed for many years. The President, still maintaining a significant silence, told the man to fill two glasses. Then he raised his own, nodded to Sachs and drank to him.

Next he remarked: 'Alex, what you are after is to see that the Nazis don't blow us up?'

'Precisely.'

It was only then that Roosevelt called in his attaché, General 'Pa' Watson, and addressed him—pointing to the two documents that Sachs had brought in — in words which have since become famous:

'Pa, this requires action!'[29]

Thus the decision was made to start the 'Manhattan Project'. It was by no means smooth sailing. It must be recalled that the United States was not at war with Germany until two years after Roosevelt made his decision. Roosevelt's ambassador to England, Joseph Kennedy, was regularly reporting that the Nazis were winning, and would win, the war. The senator from Missouri, Harry S. Truman, had gone on record as saying that: 'If we see that Germany is winning the war, we ought to help Russia, and if Russia is winning we ought to help Germany and in that way kill as many as possible.'[30] Roosevelt was one of the most popular presidents in American history, but his popularity came from below. He had many enemies in very high places just as the Nazis had many friends in those same high places.

In this context, amidst powerful isolationist impulses from both right and left, there was little enthusiasm for investing vast sums in a project whose necessity few believed in or accepted. Scientists saw no compelling reason to quit lucrative teaching and research jobs for some hare-brained scheme which they supposed the military had dreamed up. The exiled scientists were the ones who were eager to push on; but unlike England, where after some basic checks on their past, they were treated as equals, in the United States they were given a secondary status as 'aliens', and in the case of Enrico Fermi, 'enemy alien'. The British, with a higher interest at stake—they were formally at war with Germany from September 1939—and probably better informed as to what was going on inside the Nazi scientific community, were pushing ahead with their own atomic weapons project. It was news of their progress and their assessment that the A-bomb might be produced by the Nazis before the predictable end of conventional war which helped push Roosevelt's programme through. But the decision to divert substantial funds and scientific-technical resources to the Manhattan Project was only accepted in December 1941—on the *day before* Pearl Harbour.

From then it was 'bang on': the financial and technical might of the United States was mobilized and the Project was moved into high gear. Ironically, it was shortly after this that Szilard and his colleagues started to receive word from Germany that the U-Project was running into difficulties. They thus began an 'agonizing appraisal', as to whether the campaign they had waged for an American A-bomb was now justified. Their tragedy ultimately was their inability to stop the construction of the Leviathan they had originally sponsored for such understandable motives.

Mission 'Alsos'

Among the factors hampering Germany in the A-bomb race was Hitler's chronic distrust and contempt for scientists—'white Jews' as they were once described in *Das Schwarze Corps*: the weekly organ of the SS. Reciprocally, the scientists' distrust and hatred of Hitler led some of them to consciously sabotage the 'U-Project'. Another inhibiting factor was Hitler's insistence that for any new weapon to be allocated the necessary funds and resources, it had to be militarily operational within six months of approval. Massive Allied air raids were also having a devastating effect on German industry and this precluded the marshalling of the enormous resources needed to produce an A-bomb.

To learn just where the Germans were on the nuclear race-course, General Groves, Chief of the Manhattan Project, set up a commando group code-named 'Alsos'—the Greek translation of his own name—headed by Colonel Borish Pash, a top-ranking and experienced intelligence officer. Its task was to land with the first Allied troops in Europe and gather material on the German nuclear effort. He landed in Italy, but the mission was a failure because Pash lacked the scientific background to evaluate such material even when he stumbled on it. He was recalled, but sent again because Groves regarded him as an exceptionally enterprising officer. This time he was accompanied by a Dutch physicist, Samuel A. Goudsmit, whose second passion after physics was criminal investigation.

The Alsos group reached Paris with the first group of Allied troops at the end of August 1944. Goudsmit's first contact was Frédéric Joliot-Curie who, together with his wife Irène, were Nobel Prize winners and France's most outstanding physicists. Joliot-Curie's Paris laboratories had been an arsenal for the French *maquis*, mainly turning out Molotov cocktails, and the famous scientist, turned Communist during the war, had become an adept at street fighting. But he was unable to put Goudsmit onto the track of the key German scientists or what they were up to.

In November 1944, the Alsos group entered Strasbourg, hoping to capture Carl von Weizsächer. He and Werner Heisenberg, were known to be Germany's ace nuclear physicists. It was they who had proven theoretically that a reactor could be built which would substitute uranium 239 for uranium 235 in the manufacture of atomic bombs.

Goudsmit by then knew that Strasbourg had been their headquarters, but on reaching it he found that Weizsächer had left three months earlier. Rummaging through papers left behind, Goudsmit had the incredible luck of stumbling on key documents. The bundle of papers in Weizsächer's office made it unequivocally clear that the Nazis, always presumed to be in the lead, were at least two years behind Allied atomic research. They had not even begun to build the system of factories required for the production of fissionable uranium or plutonium. Apparently Albert Speer, the powerful Minister of Supply, had approved continued research and development in 1942, but restricted investment to a small scale compared with the all-out effort being mounted in the United States.

Speer's own *Memoirs* shed fascinating light on Hitler's ignorant attitude towards the German A-bomb programme. He writes that the concept of the bomb 'quite obviously strained his intellectual capacity. He was also unable to grasp the revolutionary nature of nuclear physics. In the twenty-two hundred recorded points of my conferences with Hitler, nuclear fission comes up only once, and then is mentioned with extreme brevity....' On the other hand, he adds:

> I am sure that Hitler would not have hesitated for a moment to employ atom bombs against England. I remember his reaction to the final scene of a newsreel on the bombing of Warsaw in the autumn of 1939. We were sitting with him and Goebbels in his Berlin salon watching the film. Clouds of smoke darkened the sky; dive bombers tilted and hurtled toward their goal; we could watch the flight of the released bombs, the pull-out of the planes and the cloud from the explosions expanding gigantically. The effect was enhanced by running the film in slow motion. Hitler was fascinated. The film ended with a montage showing a plane diving toward the outlines of the British Isles. A burst of flame followed, and the island flew into the air in tatters. Hitler's enthusiasm was unbounded. 'That is what will happen to them', he cried out and, carried away, 'That is how we will annihilate them!'[31]

The technical difficulties involved in the production of a German bomb began to seem insuperable by the time of the invasion of the Soviet Union in 1941, when Hitler's war industries were strained to the maximum. Speer confirms that by autumn 1941 the programme had been decisively down-graded after complaints from the scientists about technical bottlenecks and their inability to promise results for three or four years. Moreover, by the summer of 1943 wolframite imports from Portugal were halted, creating a 'critical situation for the production of solid-core ammunition. I therefore ordered the use of uranium cores for this type of ammunition.'[32] Speer's release of precious German uranium stocks precluded further serious work on a Nazi nuclear weapon.

At the time, however, the evidence discovered by Goudsmit, although it detailed the collapse of the German nuclear programme, was not regarded by Washington as conclusive. With justified suspicion, considering the stakes involved, it was conjectured that the documents might have been 'planted' to mislead and slow down Allied research. Therefore, the Alsos team was given the priority of locating Heisenberg's supposed laboratory. Goudsmit had long argued that only the brilliant Heisenberg could mastermind the Nazi project and his personal supervision would undoubtedly be necessary at every stage of development. So Goudsmit started the manhunt for his old friend from Göttingen. Eventually the Alsos mission tracked down and captured virtually the entire inner circle of the U-Project: a 'Uranium Union' comprising Heisenberg, Weizsächer, Otto Hahn and a half dozen others. Heisenberg's primitive laboratory was also located. The net result was confirmation that Germany not only had no A-bomb, it lacked the capacity to produce one.

It was then that the great lying started. At one stroke the justification for the Manhattan Project—beating the Nazis to the A-bomb—was removed and with it the moral force which Groves had invoked to spur the 150,000 men and women under his command—above all the scientists and technicians—to ever more feverish speed in their work. Groves locked the Alsos report away, marked 'top secret'. However, despite the draconian security measures in which he was so proficient, the word leaked out. The reactions of his top scientists were predictable: 'If the Germans don't have it, why should we continue?' Foremost among the questioners were the exiles, whose well-justified fears had originally galvanized the Project into existence. Groves shifted his ground, maintaining his cry of faster, ever faster by urging the need to use the bomb to force the Nazis to capitulate. In fact, his passion was to speed things up so it could be used *before* they capitulated.

Even before the Alsos group completed its investigation, Niels Bohr was worrying about the international consequences of the

United States continuing to go it alone in the race to build the Bomb. He foresaw frictions between the Allies in the post-war years and the horrifying prospect of an East-West nuclear arms race. He felt that an East-West agreement on common control of nuclear energy would be easier to arrive at before the completion of the Bomb and, above all, before its use. Almost a year before Hiroshima, Bohr personally presented his views to Roosevelt. Although there is no record of the details of their conversation, Bohr presumably reiterated the points contained in a memorandum he had sent to both Roosevelt and Churchill six weeks before. In the memorandum, Bohr had written:

> Quite apart from the question of how soon the weapon will be ready for use and what role it may play in the present way, this situation raises a number of problems which call for most urgent attention. Unless, indeed, some agreement about the use of the new active materials can be obtained in due time, any temporary advantage, however great, *may be outweighed by a perpetual menace to human security.*
>
> Ever since the possibilities of releasing atomic energy on a vast scale came in sight, much thought has naturally been given to the question of control, but the further the exploration of the scientific problems concerned is proceeding, the clearer it becomes that no kind of customary measures will suffice for this purpose, and that *the terrifying prospect of a future competition between nations about a weapon of such formidable character can only be avoided through a universal agreement in true confidence.*
>
> Without impeding the immediate military objectives, an initiative, aimed at forestalling a fateful competition, should serve *to uproot any cause of distrust between the powers on whose harmonious collaboration the fate of coming generations will depend.*[33]

After Bohr's attempt, Alexander Sachs felt that having influenced the president in his fateful decision to make the Bomb, he was duty-bound to get Roosevelt to come up with a policy decision as to the circumstances in which it would be used. He saw Roosevelt in December 1944 and, according to a version submitted to Robert B. Patterson, (then Under-Secretary of State for War), they agreed on the following formula:

> Following a successful test, there should be arranged (a) a rehear-

sal demonstration before a body including internationally recognized scientists from all Allied countries and, in addition, from neutral countries, supplemented by representatives of (religious) faiths; (b) that a report on the nature and the portent of the atomic weapon be prepared by the scientists and other representative figures; (c) that thereafter a warning be issued by the United States and its allies in the Project to our major enemies in the war, Germany and Japan, that atomic bombing would be applied to a selected area within a designated time limit for the evacuation of human and animal life; and, (d) in the wake of such realization of the efficacy of atomic bombing, an ultimatum demand for immediate surrender by the enemies be issued, in the certainty that failure to comply would subject their countries and people to atomic annihilation.[34]

Meanwhile it was becoming clear that the war in Europe would be over before the Bomb had even been tested and, by all accounts, Groves was deeply worried that there would no opportunity to demonstrate its power against a human target. Japan was still left as an enemy, but no pretence could be made that the A-bomb was necessary to preempt any Japanese nuclear programme. So a second great lie was produced out of the pack: use of the Bomb would shorten the war and save hundreds of thousands of American lives.

'Saving American lives' was later to become the nauseous formula used during the Vietnam War to justify the slaughter of women, children and even babes-in-arms at My Lai and scores of other such massacres. General Groves seems to have set the pattern with this thesis that 'saving American lives' was an acceptable justification for the murder of several hundreds of thousands of Japanese civilians. He knew also that this pretext was a lie of the first magnitude. The Bomb was not needed to secure the surrender of Japan. When the word filtered through Groves's 'tight' security system that the Bomb would be tested and then speedily used against Japan, there was a revolt among the scientists. And, as had been the case when they knew that Germany was no longer in the race, those most concerned were the ones who had been the first advocates of the Manhattan project. Thus Szilard and Franck found themselves in the vanguard of the rebellious project scientists. Szilard tried to repeat his feat of 1941, first eliciting a support letter from Einstein and then preparing a letter and memorandum for President Roosevelt. Both were found unopened on the President's desk after his death in April 1945. The next move was to approach Secretary Robert Patterson.

A memorandum was submitted on 11 June 1945, signed by those who became famous as the 'Chicago Seven': Franck, Szilard, Hogness, Rabinowitch, Nicholson, Seaborg and Hughes. It is a long document, setting forth in an objective manner the various options open to the United States arising from its monopoly of the A-bomb. Realistic and prophetic, the document pleads, as did Bohr, for an international agreement prior to any use of the Bomb. Some passages are worth quoting:

> Thus, from the 'optimistic' point of view—looking forward to an international agreement on the prevention of nuclear warfare—the military advantages and the saving of American lives achieved by the sudden use of atomic bombs against Japan may be outweighed by the ensuing loss of confidence and by a wave of horror and repulsion sweeping over the rest of the world and perhaps even dividing public opinion at home. From this point of view, a demonstration of the new weapon might best be made, before the eyes of representatives of the United Nations, on the desert or a barren island...

This impassioned but logical and well-argued plea ends with the summary:

> Nuclear bombs cannot possibly remain a 'secret weapon' at the exclusive disposal of this country for more than a few years. The scientific facts on which construction is based are well known to scientists of other countries. Unless an effective international control of nuclear explosives is instituted, a race for nuclear armaments is certain to ensue following the first revelation of nuclear weapons to the world....
>
> We believe that these considerations make the use of nuclear bombs, for an early and unannounced attack against Japan, inadvisable. If the United States were to be the first to release this new means of indiscriminate destruction upon mankind, she would

sacrifice public support throughout the world, precipitate the race for armaments and prejudice the possibility of an international agreement on the future control of such weapons...[35]

This powerful plea was ignored. Truman replaced Roosevelt as president and his viewpoint had little changed since the time, at the beginning of the war, when he expressed the hope that the Russians and Germans would kill each other off. Meanwhile the war against Japan was approaching its climax, the island-hopping operations having secured the last stepping stones to Japan itself. In the fierce month-long battle for Iwo Jima in February-March 1945 the US Marines took 21,000 casualties. The capture of this strategic island brought American naval and air power within 700 miles of Tokyo. By the beginning of July, the northward advance of MacArthur's forces had finally secured Okinawa at an even heavier cost. Between Iwo Jima, Okinawa and Japan, there were no more military obstacles of any consequence. Japanese naval and air power had been almost totally wiped out. I participated with the aircraft carriers in the battles for Iwo Jima and Okinawa, landing at Okinawa only for the final stage of mopping-up operations. I had many conversations with senior US naval, marine and army officers during those battles. It was an open secret that the final great operation would be a combined Army and Marine landing in Japan itself scheduled for 1 November 1945. The admirals and colonels with whom I spoke were confident that Japan would be taken, even at enormous cost, but they were gloomy at the prospects after that.

The great question, central to all our conversations at that time, was whether Stalin would respect his pledge to deal with the Japanese on mainland China. The Japanese Kwantung Army was considered an elite force, virtually untouched by the war and with a powerful heavy industry base in Manchuria. The prevailing opinion was that the Soviet Army would not be attacked. 'Why should they?' argued one task force admiral with whom I had daily conversations in between battles. 'It would suit them down to the ground to see us bogged down in a land war on the Asian mainland.' Another, who conceded that Stalin had been correct in maintaining his military timetables, said: 'But if they do move, how will we ever get them out of mainland China? Better fight the Japs now than the Russkies later.' Although at the time it was unlikely that any of them were aware of the A-bomb's existence—its development being held secret from even the most senior commanders—it was the ideal solution to their quandary over Russian-intervention. Based on many conversations I could imagine the glee with which the use of the Bomb against Hiroshima was greeted.

It was interesting that on the uss *Bennington*—one of the aircraft carriers involved in the Iwo Jima landings and later in the first carrier-based air attacks against Japan—my inveterate battlefield companion, Bill McGaffin of the *Chicago Daily News*, and I shared the admiral's suite with the playwright Robert Sherwood, a member of Roosevelt's 'brains trust'. Together with Harry Hopkins, he was one of those personally closest to Roosevelt. A delightful, humane and witty man, it was a great pleasure to be in his company. The admiral's quarters were free because Sherwood's official travelling companion was the Secretary of the Navy, James Forrestal,[36] who was travelling on the flagship of the task force commander. One thing intrigued us about Sherwood. He spent much of his time questioning officers, crewmen and pilots—also McGaffin and myself—as to the reaction if some powerful, non-conventional weapon was used to shorten the war with Japan. Most of us assumed he was probably talking about poison gas, and the response was virtually unanimous: 'Anything to end this war and get us home.' It was a predictable attitude. It was not surprising that American servicemen had few tender feelings towards the Japanese military after four years of combat and brutality on both sides. My own deepest desire was to see the war ended, to get out of my war correspondent's military uniform and back to civilian life. I think these were the reactions of McGaffin and myself to the use of what we supposed were some secret war-winning weapons for use against military targets on the beach-heads and battlefields.

In the first days of June 1945, after the deliberations of a presidential hand-packed 'Interim Committee' on the use of A-bombs, a recommendation was sent to President Truman:

(a) The Bomb should be used against Japan as soon as possible.
(b) It should be used on a dual target—that is an installation or war plant surrounded by, or adjacent to, houses and other buildings most susceptible to damage.
(c) It should be used without prior warning of the nature of the weapon.

Point (c) was a condensed version of a point (d) in an earlier stipulation by Groves that: 'the first target should be, if possible one that has escaped earlier bombardments, so that the effect of a single atomic bomb can be ascertained.' This was the reason why in broadcast warnings to the Japanese people, Hiroshima and Nagasaki were not included in the list of seventeen cities to be subject to conventional bombing!

On 16 July the bomb was successfully tested at Alamogordo and preparations were accelerated for its use against a Japanese city. The final decision was obviously that of President Truman. When he made it, he knew that the war with Japan was as good as over. During the Potsdam Conference Stalin had shown Truman a message he had just received from Moscow. (It seems that Truman already knew about it from us intelligence intercepts of cable traffic.) It announced the imminent arrival of Japan's former prime minister, Prince Fumijaro Konoye, in Moscow on 12 July for talks on how to end the war. The essential part of the message was that: 'His Majesty the Emperor is greatly concerned over the daily increasing casualties and sacrifices faced by the citizens of the various countries in this present war, and it is His Majesty's heart's desire to see the swift termination of this War... and so it is His Majesty's earnest hope that peace may be restored as speedily as possible for the welfare of mankind.'[37]

Stripped of phoney moralistic rhetoric, this was an offer to surrender. Stalin asked Truman whether it merited a reply and Truman's response was negative. One might well ask what had happened to the dedication to 'save American lives'? Truman had been informed via Portugal over a month earlier that Japan was ready for peace talks with a proviso that 'unconditional surrender' would not be acceptable and that the home islands would remain ' in Japan's possession.[38]

Truman's reaction was to insist on what he knew to be totally unacceptable—that is, 'unconditional surrender' in terms which made it clear that he was demanding the head of Emperor Hirohito. Moreover he did this in an underhand way which violated the elementary codes of international diplomacy. An ultimatum was sent to Japan from Potsdam phrased as a joint declaration of the three major Allied powers. In fact the Russians were not consulted and learned of the three-power ultimatum only after it had been broadcast to the world. It was a monumental piece of deceit which, even more than Churchill's famous 'Iron Curtain' speech eight months later, marked the real beginning of the Cold War. Moreover it was a classic example of the kind of diplomacy by corporation lawyers,—disingenuous and self-righteous—that characterized the Truman Administration. What happened has been excellently summarized by D. F. Fleming:

> When Russia did declare war on Japan, on August 8, the Moscow correspondent of the *New York Times* cabled that he had heard months ago that Russia would enter the war on Japan three months after VE day, and both the military expert of the *Times* and the editor stated plainly, on the 9th, that they had known about the Yalta Agreement. Churchill also testified in his address of August 16 that he knew Russia's entry was due on August 8... Effective use of the bomb depended on dropping it either before Russia's entry into the war or immediately afterwards. A dramatic warning was to be issued from Potsdam by '*all* of Japan's principal enemies'. Actually this term included Russia since she was pledged to war with Japan, but technically and legally she could be ignored and the warning issued without her knowledge.
>
> Secretary of State Byrnes has given the details. Secretary Stimson had informed the American leaders that the July 16 test of the A-bomb had met our highest hopes and on the evening of July 26, in the midst of the Potsdam Conference, a telegramme arrived from Chiang Kai-shek, approving the test of the ultimatum to Japan, thereafter known as the Potsdam Declaration. The declaration, says Byrnes, 'was immediately released for publication and a copy was sent by special messenger to Molotov.' Later in the evening, Molotov telephoned asking that the declaration be held up two or

three days. When he was told that it had already been released he seemed disturbed. The next day Byrnes explained to Molotov that the declaration had not been presented to him because we did not want to embarrass the Soviet Union since it was not yet at war with Japan. Molotov said simply that we should have consulted him. The impression in Molotov's mind would be doubly strong since Stalin had twice told Truman and Byrnes, earlier in the conference, about successive efforts on Japan's part to enlist Russia as a mediator and his failure to encourage that idea. President Truman expressed his approval of Stalin's action.[39]

Referring to the sudden change of the position of the United States and Britain from their previous urgent insistence that the Soviet Union enter the war with Japan and deal with the two million Japanese troops on the Chinese mainland, Fleming reports that this was highly embarrassing to Truman and Byrnes once they learned that the A-bomb had been successfully tested. 'Byrnes believed the atomic bomb would be successful,' indicating that he expected that the Japanese would reject the Potsdam ultimatum.... The same idea had been expressed to Mikolajczyk[40] on 15 June. Relating that Stalin had asked for the Potsdam Conference because he wanted to get into the Japanese war, Churchill said: '"We don't care whether he comes into the war against the Japanese or not. We don't need him now."'[41]

Predictably, Japan's Prime Minister Suzuki rejected the ultimatum as unworthy of public attention. 'Little Boy' and 'Fat Man' had already been rushed to Tinien Island (in the Marianas group), and assembled for detonation against Hiroshima and Nagasaki on 6 and 9 August respectively.

6
Bitter Harvest

The Chicago Seven's warning about the risk of a 'wave of horror and repulsion sweeping over the rest of the world and perhaps even dividing public opinion at home was immediately justified. The ensuing moral fallout was dramatized by the case of Major Claude Eatherly who had piloted the plane which gave the 'all clear' signal for the *Enola Gay* to drop the bomb on Hiroshima.

After landing his B-29 on Tinian, Eatherly retreated into silence and depression, speaking to no one for days. His condition was diagnosed as 'battle fatigue' and he was shipped home. For a while after being discharged, Eatherly seemed to settle quietly back into family life. But at night terrible images of an inferno tormented the ex-pilot. After a while a few drinks were no longer sufficient to banish his nightmares, and severe insomnia and depression began to set in, leading to Eatherly's first suicide attempt in a New Orleans hotel room in 1950. Voluntarily, he entered a military mental hospital in Waco, Texas for six months of treatment without any apparent improvement in his depression. After his release he again tried to take his life and his wife threatened divorce unless he re-entered the hospital.

Waving aside the agonizing crisis of conscience with which Eatherly was gripped, the doctors at Waco treated his case as simply another pathological syndrome, marked by a 'fear complex', and prescribed a massive programme of insulin injections. The insulin treatment initially seemed to allay the symptoms, and Eatherly rejoined his wife. Inexorably, however, he again relapsed—even stealing money to send to Hiroshima. In the end his wife divorced him and had him barred from visiting their children. He became a notorious 'case', his ups and downs reported in the press, and, in 1959, this publicity attracted the attention of a well-known philosopher, Günther Anders. Anders was immediately struck by the expiatory quality of Eatherly's suffering and initiated a correspondence with him, urging the former pilot to start fighting back against the system which, by conscripting him to a mission of genocide, had ruined his life.

As a gradual result of his correspondence and friendship with Anders, Eatherly became a 'peacenik' in the most difficult conditions. Like the example of the *hibakusha* which I mentioned earlier, the act of resistance had a healing effect, bringing a new hope and sense of purposefulness. He struck up a moving correspondence with some of the *hibakusha* themselves, and his messages to the people of Hiroshima became known world-wide. Meanwhile, Anders won Eatherly over to the project of writing a book about his experiences and how they transformed his life. With increasing confidence, Eatherly looked forward to this challenge and to his release.

Yet as Eatherly, with Anders's constant support, attempted to arouse public attention to the legacy of Hiroshima and Nagasaki, he became more of an official 'nuisance' and was subjected to increasingly harsh and petty disciplinary retaliation by the Veterans' Administration. Various agencies applied pressure on his brother not to facilitate Eatherly's release, with the result that the brother ultimately refused to sign the 'responsibility form' which automatically would have set him free. The political motivation in his brother's act, and a measure of the political pressure applied, is clear from the repeated urgings to Eatherly to stop writing or making any statements about his anti-war feelings.

Faced with the prospect of indefinite commitment to Waco, Eatherly decided to escape from his Kafka-esque situation:

Dear Günther,
 I am very sorry that I have not written you sooner, but I have been trying to get out of the hospital legally with lawyers. That failed because the Air Force filed a commitment against me indefinite-

ly, and then had the hospital notify the court not to serve a summons on me so I could not take it to court. Last Wednesday I talked with my doctor and he told me I was in the unfortunate position of being so well-known and famous, that I must stop my writings about nuclear weapons and using my influence in foreign countries through US magazines. He said that he could do nothing to help me, that he and the hospital staff had to take orders from the Air Force and the State Department. I asked him if they intended to keep me here, and he said yes.

So I made arrangements for friends to help me once outside. I eloped from the hospital... So now I have to stay up in a very nice apartment... I cannot leave because the Government has everyone on the lookout for me... Günther, I hope you don't think I am foolish for trying to escape that... I will work this out... so don't be worried. I have so many people who are working to protect me...[42]

Two months later, Eatherly was spotted by a policeman while a passenger in a car. Much attention was given in the press to his escape and recapture. Hauled before a jury, and denounced by military 'experts', he was recommitted, indefinitely, to Waco. This time, however, Eatherly was assigned to the section of the hospital where the violently insane were kept.

A Mr Ray Bell, reporter for the Waco *News Tribune*, who had established contact with Eatherly's lawyer, meanwhile wrote to Anders, expressing his horror at the court proceedings and the treatment of Eatherly. 'Quite frankly, I was most surprised at the jury's verdict on 12 January and more than a little moved at the sheer stupidity it reflected.... And it does seem rather absurd for any man, psychiatrist or not, to state that he can tell a man's mental condition merely by shaking his hand.... Frankly, I feel this is one of the most significant stories of our generation, and, who knows, perhaps of all generations....'[43] In reply, Anders pointed to a recent article by Bertrand Russell in the *New Statesman* in which the great English philosopher proclaimed: 'If the one who wrote them [referring to some of Eatherly's letters to Anders] is considered mad, then I shall not be surprised if my last years are spent in a lunatic asylum—where I shall enjoy the company of all who are capable of feelings of humanity.'[44]

America Kills Its Own

The Eatherly case was rather like a Dreyfus Affair of the nuclear age, demonstrating the lengths to which the US government was prepared to go to cover up the question of guilt for the atomic holocausts of August 1945. But it was unique only in the tragic heroism of Eatherly's persistence in fighting the system, and the international support which his struggle attracted. Other American victims of the bomb—both moral and physical—have passed officially unnoticed at the time, their plight—like that of the immeasurably larger number of Japanese *hibakusha*—recognized only years later. For instance, in August 1945, while the nuclear wizards of Los Alamos celebrated the 'success' of the Manhattan Project in a month-long round of cocktail parties, a young researcher, Harry Dagnian, was slowly dying an agonizing death as a result of an atomic chain reaction which he had accidentally set-off in a minute quantity of fissile material. Because the official War Department policy as we have seen, denied the dangers of radiation poisoning, his illness was disguised by his own best friends who were forced, under military order, to continue the cocktail circuit, pretending that everything was absolutely fine. Meanwhile the effects of gamma ray radiation were devastating Dagnian's internal organs. He died in great pain twenty-four days after initial exposure. (In one Congressional hearing, General Groves, finally cornered on the question of radiation deaths, attempted to reassure congressmen that it was a 'very pleasant' way to go!)

For thirty years the United States government persisted in its policy of covering up the radiation after-effects of the test bombs, as well as the Hiroshima and Nagasaki *hibakusha*. Incredibly, even after the dangers had been extensively studied, the Defense Department continued to use its own troops as guinea-pigs in above-ground tests of atomic and hydrogen bombs. The scale of the cover-up involved was disclosed in the Washington *Post* on 8 April 1983, under the banner, 'VA Agrees to Free Medical Care for GIs Exposed to US A-Tests':

> After seventeen months of delay, the Veterans Administration has

agreed to give medical treatment to military personnel who took part in open-air atomic tests whose illness might have been caused by exposure to radiation. The policy change, announced at a meeting of the Senate Veterans Affairs Committee Wednesday, was a belated victory for the nation's 'atomic veterans'—an estimated 250,000 to 500,000 serviceman who participated in atomic tests in Nevada and the Pacific between 1945 and 1962. Free medical care brings the veterans one step closer to obtaining the same limited rights that the VA had granted reluctantly to Vietnam veterans exposed to the defoliant, Agent Orange.

But officials said the agency does not intend to soften its policy of rejecting most disability claims filed by atomic veterans. VA scientists said they do not believe there is any evidence that those blems.... Congress ordered the VA in 1981 to provide free health care to veterans for any ailment that might reasonably be assumed to result from exposure to radiation or to Agent Orange. The VA began providing such care to veterans exposed to Agent Orange but it limited treatment for 'atomic veterans' to those suffering from cancer or thyroid diseases.

A parade of witnesses, mostly from the National Association of Atomic Veterans, denounced the VA for failing to enact standard procedures for deciding when 'atomic veterans' should receive disability compensation. A total of 2,067 'atomic veterans' have filed claims for a variety of disabilites that they blame on exposure to radiation. The VA has approved 29 of them, including 29 on appeal.

These American *hibakusha* discovered to their astonishment that they had to wage a bitter struggle, like their Japanese counterparts, to get even medical treatment. And, like the Utah sheep ranchers whose claims for compensation had the same origin, they were the victims of what a belated court judgement regarding the ranchers characterized as 'governmental fraud and deceit'. In fact the majority of the 'atomic veterans' could also be considered as victims of the Korean War. The tests in which they participated were essentially to establish conditions in which ground troops could advance into enemy territory and occupy the terrain, immediately after their opponents had been subjected to nuclear bombardment. An untold number of Americans died because of this and an unknowable number will die in the future. Doubtless they will be written off as 'expendable' in the sacred interest of 'saving American lives'.

In an Introduction to Howard Rosenberg's *Atomic Soldiers*, Jack Anderson, the American columnist famous for his irreverent attitude towards the Washington Establishment, writes of the great illusion that the USA could retain monopoly of nuclear weaponry. Shattered by the USSR's explosion of *its* Bomb:

> The federal custodians of the terrible secret responded to the danger with a strange schizophrenia. On the one hand they began protecting their secret with a quite almost paranoiac panic. They tried by edict to cram the genie back into the bottle. They banned all discussion and speculation about the atomic bomb. The censorship directive covered everything from the bomb's workings and postwar usage, to international agreements and possible medical applications... They became suspicious even of the scientists who had developed the bomb. This presented an awkward dilemma: how could the federal guardians withhold the atomic secret from the scientists who had created it? The attempt was made nonetheless, using oppressive security regulations and witch hunts. To this day, the American people remain in official darkness about the lethal fallout from the atomic-bomb tests of the 1950s. Disquieting questions were raised about atmospheric testing, and disturbing consequences were chronicled. But these were summarily suppressed...
>
> The history of nuclear power has been plagued with too much haste, which has created incalculable dangers, and overzealous secrecy, which has concealed the truth from the endangered populace.[45]

A major part of that concealed truth was the radiation effects on unknown thousands of American troops who took part in the preparations for the use of tactical A-bombs in Korea and the further perfecting of the strategic H-bombs. In their haste to use the A-bombs in Korea, the military authorities, camouflaged under the name of the Atomic Energy Commission, were using Americans as guinea-pigs.

If the United States agreed to start ceasefire talks to end the fighting in Korea, it was only because there was a battlefield stalemate along a line roughly where the war had started. Costly efforts for the Americans to push north of that line had failed. Now it has become clear that the interminable delays and interruptions in the talks were to gain time while techniques were developed to adapt A-bombs for battlefield conditions. The speed-up started with the outbreak of hostilities in Korea. Thus notes, author Rosenberg, 'Time was a luxury the atom-bomb testing programme did not have in 1950. US troops had landed in Korea in July and forced the invading North Koreans back above the 38th parallel dividing the two countries. But the battles were costly, and by November 1950, General Douglas MacArthur, commander of UN forces in Korea, reported that Chinese Communist troops were fighting as proxies of the North Koreans. At AEC headquarters in Washington, urgency was a prime factor in deciding where and when to resume the bomb testing programme.'[46]

The choice fell on the Tonopah Bombing and Gunnery Range near Las Vegas in Nevada. It was recognized that there would be a great outcry if it became known that American troops were being subjected to tests, involving radiation risks, so military advisers, who dominated the AEC, noted in a memo that: 'Not only must high safety facts be established in fact, but the *acceptance of these facts by the general public must be ensured by the judicious handling of the public information programme.*'[47]

But the safety standards adopted at the beginning of the tests, on 27 January 1951, were gradually lowered as battlefield needs became more urgent. At one of the tests code-named 'Buster-Jangle', all three branches of the armed services demanded that they be carried out in more realistic conditions, with combat troops taking part in at least one of the test series. Thus was taken the first fateful step to deliberately expose US troops to atomic radiation and ascertain 'how much they could take'. The next step was to move them closer and closer to the epicentre of the explosion, with an ever-faster follow-up in simulated assaults against the 'enemy positions'. Some of the AEC leaders became alarmed at the scandal which would ensue if the agreed safety standards were violated. An argument developed between the military and civilian representatives and between the AEC and the Pentagon. It ended with the AEC saying in effect: 'If you insist in doing it your way, then you assume full responsibility.' To which the military with the AEC saying in effect: 'If you insist in doing it your way, then you assume full responsibility.' To which the military replied: 'Thanks very much, we will.' So they assumed what inevitably turned out to be full '*irresponsibility*' for what led to the present argument with the Veterans Administration.

A byproduct of the testing of H-weapons was that radio active fall-out made its appearance as far away as New York, with a marked increase in leukemia, liver cancer and other typical forms of radiation sickness. Rosenberg comments that: 'Slowly but sure-ly, the Commission abdicated virtually all of its safety and health responsibilities, to the Pentagon. And that was a mistake.'[48] In all the early claims of compensations from human sufferers and the ranchers who lost sheep, cattle and horses, the official defence was 'there is no way of proving that these effects were due to exposure to radiation.'

7

Hiroshima and the Cold War

The fate that befell Claude Eatherly, one day a hero of the 'Victory Boys' (as the A-bomber group was known), the next an outcast and villain, was symbolic of what happened to the Soviet Union. One day the 'gallant ally', the next an unwanted pariah in the eyes of the Western Allies. Churchill's remarks to Mikolajczyk that it was Stalin 'who had asked for the Potsdam Conference because he wanted to get into the Japanese war' was a gross untruth and Churchill knew this. The truth was the opposite. The AP White House correspondent who accompanied Truman to Potsdam, was quoted in the *New York Times* on 9 August 1945: 'Final agreement on Russia's entry into the war with Japan, it may now be disclosed, was the "primary objective" of President Truman's participation in the Potsdam Conference. A Soviet declaration of war, the President said, might save hundreds of thousands of Americans from injury or death. Leaning against a rail of the *Augusta*, en route to Europe, he frequently remarked on the job ahead. 'I want more than anything else,' he said, 'the use of Russian air bases with which to step up the assault on Japan and its conquered territories.' But as we have seen the news that the A-bomb had been successfully tested diametrically changed Truman's attitude, with Churchill heartily applauding on the sidelines.

Four days after Emperor Hirohito's broadcast accepting defeat and willingness to surrender, the United States halted all land-lease shipments to the Soviet Union, including urgently needed food and transport equipment for civilian relief, thus serving notice that the 'gallant ally' not only was no longer needed but had to be punished, ostensibly for having obtained agreement on spheres of influence and security at the Yalta Conference in exchange for the urgently requested pledge to deal with Japan's two million strong army in mainland China. Hiroshima tempted Truman to repudiate that agreement and to reverse the entire Rooseveltian concept of continuing cooperation with the Soviet Union in the postwar period. His famous 'roll back' policy started to take shape. In language which strikingly prefigured President Reagan's dangerous blusterings nearly four decades later, Truman began to speak of the 'forces of evil', and the 'loftier moral' purposes of the United States. Thus at a Navy Day speech on 27 October, Truman announced that there could be 'no compromise with the forces of evil' and enunciated twelve principles all of them of 'the highest moral and democratic principles as we understand them' (sic). (It has struck many reporters of the American scene, especially those who were around in the late 1940s, how uncannily Reagan's new cold war resembles Truman's 'old' cold war, even down to the oratory in which they are presented and defended).

Just ninety days after the first A-bomb was used, we find Truman affirming that the 'atomic bombs which fell on Hiroshima and Nagasaki must be a signal, not for the old process of falling apart—but for an era of ever closer unity and ever closer friendship among peaceful nations ... this new power of destruction we regard as a sacred trust.' The concept of the 'goodies' versus the 'baddies' was thus firmly launched. It was the sort of hypocritical nonsense that Reagan was later to use in justifying his 'star war' fantasies to ensure victory in the struggle 'between right and wrong, good and evil' and check the 'aggressive impulses of an evil empire'.[49]

One would have to reverse all the concepts of 'good and evil', as they are taught in the churches of any denominations, to accept what was done to Japan's A-bombed and fire-bombed cities as 'good', and the revulsion to this as 'evil'. Or, to accept as 'good' the lies which Truman and his top political and military aides used to justify the extermination of hundreds of thousands of Japanese civilians in order to geopolitically project the might of the American nuclear monopoly. That this was the intention was revealed by then Secretary of War, Henry Stimson, as summarized by the historian, Barton Bernstein.'

> Both Secretary of War Stimson and Secretary of State James F. Byrnes had foreseen the importance of the bomb to American foreign policy. To Stimson it had long promised to be a 'master card' for diplomacy. After Hiroshima and Nagasaki *Byrnes was eager to use the bomb as at least an 'implied threat'* in negotiations with Russia, and Truman seems to have agreed on a vigorous course in trying to roll back Russian influence in Eastern Europe... In his report on the Potsdam Conference the day after the second bomb, the President asserted that Rumania, Bulgaria, and Hungary 'are not to be spheres of influence of any one power' and at the same time proclaimed that the United States would be the 'trustees' of the atomic bomb. At the same time with his typical use of double standards based on his presumption of many years of nuclear weapons monopoly, he demanded all matters affecting the West should be settled 'without interference from outside the Western Hemisphere'.[50]

Even Stimson, who had been hawkish enough in his enthusiasm for using the monopoly on the a-bomb as a lever in negotiations with the Soviet Union, began to have second thoughts as the time approached for his retirement and replacement by his Undersecretary for War Robert Patterson. And William Laurence had noted with at least assumed alarm that the world was still thinking in terms of further use of the A-bomb (although against 'whom', he did not specify). He described discussions within Truman's Cabinet as being 'truly amazing', to the extent they had concentrated solely on whether the secrets of nuclear weaponry should be shared with the Soviet Union, and that no one in authority had proposed that the A-bomb be completely banned from use in war. Stimson, despite his ultra-conservative views, was a man of some vision and intelligence; Secretary of State Byrnes, on the other hand, was not only a superhawk, but a man of limited intelligence and still more limited vision. He is reported to have been convinced that the United States would retain a monopoly on nuclear weapons for at least seven years and insisted on conducting a foreign policy offensive based on that assumption.

D.F. Fleming notes that after Stimson's return from the Potsdam Conference and a long period of rest and reflection in the Adirondacks mountains he came to re-appraise his own position and that of the Truman administration regarding nuclear weapons and the Soviet Union. His conclusion was that his own 'life-long policy of making a man trustworthy by trusting him should be applied to the Russians.'

> He therefore submitted to President Truman, on 11 September 1945, a memorandum which is one of the most significant documents of that memorable year. Stimson pointed out that 'unless the Soviets are voluntarily invited into the partnership upon a basis of cooperation and trust' a desperate arms race would result. He considered satisfactory relations with Russia to be 'virtually dominated by the problem of the atomic bomb.' It was vital to make sure that when they did get it, they would be willing and cooperative partners. Our relations might be 'perhaps irretrievably embittered by the way in which we approach the solution of the bomb with Russia. For if we fail to approach them now and merely continue to negotiate with them, having this weapon rather ostentatiously on our hip, their suspicions and their distrust of our motives and purposes will increase.' It would inspire them to all-out efforts to solve the problems themselves.
>
> It was his judgement that the Russians would be more likely to respond to a direct and forthright approach from the United States. He emphasized 'perhaps beyond all other considerations the importance of taking this action with Russia—backed by Great Britain but peculiarly the proposal of the United States. Action of any international group of nations, including many small nations who have not demonstrated their potential power of responsibility in this war would not, in my opinion, be taken seriously by the Soviets...'
>
> As the outline of a direct approach to the Kremlin, Stimson suggested that the Big Three agree to stop all work on atomic bombs, that those which we had be impounded, and that an agreement be made never to use the A-bomb in war unless all three governments agreed to do so.

This programme for seeking agreement with the Russians early and directly—it was only a month after Hiroshima—was advanced by the ablest elder statesman in the President's Cabinet. Stimson had been Secretary of War and Secretary of State in troubled periods before he headed the War Department throughout our greatest war. If anyone was entitled to be listened to in his last public endeavour, he was the man. At the last Cabinet meeting he attended, on 21 September 1945, the day of his retirement, he urgently expressed the same views—prompt effort to achieve control of atomic warfare by direct negotiations with the Russians ...

However, the Joint Chiefs of Staff recommended that the United States 'retain all existing secrets with respect to the atomic weapons,' and of course the Stimson approach was never tried. Truman 'respected and trusted Stimson' but not to the extent of trusting the Russians.

Two years later Stimson thought that the chances of success were less than he had anticipated, but he still believed that "the existence of any chance at all would have justified the attempt, so great was the objective at stake." By 1950 this seemed truer still. By then the policy of distrusting the Russians, and insisting on the ultimate of guarantees, had been repaid in distrust, brash and vituperative, many times over.[51]

The rejection of the wise counsel of Stimson brought about exactly the consequences he had warned against, and other presidents following the policies initiated by Truman, have steered the world into the intolerable situation in which we find ourselves today. The power of the bomb gave birth to an unprecedented arrogance among both the military and the civilian policy-makers. The American military plane on which I flew back from the United States to England after the war's end was loaded with officers on their way to occupation duties in Germany. As I was still in my war correspondent's uniform—war correspondents towards the end of the war had the 'assimilated' rank of major or lieutenant-commander—the American officers took me automatically for a buddy. Their views were virtually 'his master's voice' replicas of Truman's. 'It's the American century, we've got the power and we'll goddam well use it. We've dealt with the Germans and Japs now we'll show the Russkies where they get off'—and similar expressions of nuclear swashbucklery. This was only a foretaste of what I was to see during the next three and a quarter years in Berlin, still as a correspondent of the *Daily Express*, as such concepts became official US policy in dealing with the Soviet Union in the four-power administration of Germany.

This line of thought was given official benediction by Winston Churchill in his notorious Fulton speech, which many contemporary historians—wrongly in my view—mark as the beginning of the 'Cold War'. In fact, it started nine months earlier from the minute that Truman received the 'It's a boy' message during the Potsdam Conference. The Fulton speech inaugurated Churchill's own crusade, now as Tory Opposition leader, to encourage Truman to escalate the Cold War. Given Truman's own meagre status as 'world statesman', Churchill's almost mythic stature in America (after years of adulation in the press) was an invaluable asset in the battle radically to shift public opinion from friendship to enmity with the Soviet Union. The speech itself was blunt about the shape of things to come. After giving lip service to the United Nations and the necessity of 'immediately providing it with an international armed force', Churchill warned:

> It would nevertheless be wrong and imprudent to entrust the secret knowledge or experience of the atomic bomb, which the United States, Britain and Canada now share, to the World Organization while it is still in its infancy. It would be criminal madness to cast it adrift in this still agitated and un-united world. No one in any country has slept less well in their beds because this knowledge, and the methods and raw materials to apply it, are at present largely retained in American hands. I do not believe we should all have slept so soundly had the position been reversed and some Communist or neo-fascist state monopolized for the time being these dreadful agencies. The fear of them alone might easily have been used to enforce totalitarian systems upon the free, democratic world, with consequences appalling to human imagination. God has willed that this should not be, and we have at least a breathing space before this peril has to be encountered, and even then, if no effort is spared, we should still possess so formidable a superiority, as to impose effective deterrents upon its employment or threat of

employment by others...

In case it was not clear to his listeners and those who would read at least, excerpts, of the speech in virtually every newspaper and magazine in the western world, Churchill went on to extol the virtues of the English-speaking world, its conceptions of liberty and democratic traditions in terms to which no one could take much exception. He spoke of the need for 'a special relationship between the British Commonwealth Empire and the United States . ... the continuance of the present facilities for mutual security by the joint use of naval and air force bases in the possession of either country all over the world....' (This was the policy later to be known as 'interdependence'.) Then he came to the passage which won him the unenviable fame of having ideologically fathered the 'Cold War'. The 'gallant ally'—the invariable phrase used by Churchill in referring to the Soviet Union during the war—had now become a dangerous heretic to be burned at the stake.

> A shadow has fallen upon the scenes so lately lighted by the Allied victory. Nobody knows what Soviet Russia and its Communist international organization intends to do in the immediate future or what are the limits, if any, to their expansive and proselytizing tendencies...
>
> From Stettin on the Baltic to Trieste on the Adriatic an iron curtain has descended across the Continent. Behind that line lie all the capitals of the ancient States of Central and Eastern Europe— Warsaw, Berlin, Prague, Vienna, Budapest, Belgrade, Bucharest and Sofia. All these famous cities and the populations around them lie in the Soviet sphere, and all are subject in one form or another not only to Soviet influence, but to a very high and increasing measure of control from Moscow. Athens alone, with its immortal glories, is free to decide its future at an election under British, American and French observation...[52]

And so on. In fact the spheres of influence had been agreed by Churchill, Roosevelt and Stalin at the Yalta Conference. It was the Soviet Army which, in cooperation with mainly weak local resistance forces had liberated them from Nazi occupation. All of the countries of which Churchill had named the capitals had sent troops to fight with the Nazis inside the Soviet Union. At the same time, American total casualties (killed or missing in action) for all war theatres was officially stated as just under 400,000; British killed and missing in action for all three services, including the Home Guard and other auxiliary services, were almost exactly the same as those of the United States. The nearest estimate of total casualties for the Soviet Union is twenty million. These figures reflect the proportionate contributions which each of the three main allies made in defeating the Axis powers. The spheres of influence were intended as temporary measures to ensure the security of the three main allies—France later being brought in as having suffered three invasions from Germany in less than a century.

That there was an 'iron curtain' drawn across Europe, no one could deny nor can any informed observer deny that this was, at least in part, due to Truman's declared policy, to 'roll-back' Soviet influence from the spheres agreed on at the Yalta Conference. Churchill's use of Greece as a model was ill-chosen, to say the least. Stalin had agreed at Yalta that Greece could be included in the British sphere of influence. British occupation troops immediately started militarily suppressing the Greek resistance movement which had so heroically fought against the Nazi occupation. As to the elections, they were a farce; the British supporting former Nazi collaborators and arresting the anti-Nazi resistance leaders. I was expelled from Greece, with British approval, immediately following the elections on 31 March 1946, for reporting what I had seen in Salonika and in Greek Macedonia; also for predicting that civil war was bound to break out. The policy of the Left, including EAM which represented the anti-Nazi resistance movement, was to boycott the elections. But I saw village after village surrounded by the British-backed Greek Army, escorting those of voting age to the polls and shooting those who tried to escape the army cordons. I went into prisons the day following the balloting (the authorities believing I was a UN 'observer') and talked with those who had been wounded by rifle fire or beaten unconscious for trying to avoid voting. One of those with whom I talked had a high British decoration for his wartime activities. After my report was splashed across the front-page of the *Daily*

Express I was served with an expulsion order. The reaction of the British Consul in Salonika was that 'it served me right and he could do nothing to help me.' So I did not find an 'Athens alone... free to decide its future at an election under British, American and French observation...'

The Greek civil war, in which the United States was to use napalm against Europeans for the first time, broke out almost immediately. Meanwhile over the protests of some of America's most brilliant scientists and intellectuals, the Truman administration rushed ahead with Edward Teller's 'Super' Project: the production of the Hydrogen Bomb. Since the 'implied threat' of the A-bomb against the USSR had not had the desired deterrent effect in rolling-back Yalta, Washington felt an even bigger stick was necessary. Meanwhile, as the Americans were to discover to their chagrin in August 1949, comrade Kurchatov had been taking seriously Stalin's Potsdam order 'to get a move on with our work'.

The Nuclear Hawks at Berlin

1949 was a bad year for the nuclear war zealots with whom Truman had surrounded himself—and even worse for those super-zealots who had been waiting in the wings to replace him. He was accused of not having pressed home quickly enough the advantages conferred by the US monopoly of nuclear weapons, and there were still no signs of 'roll-back'. It had been taken for granted, however, by the 'hawks' with whom General Lucius Clay, Truman's Proconsul in Germany, had staffed his headquarters, that the Republican candidate, Thomas Dewey, would win the 1948 presidential elections and then the nuclear sparks would start to fly.

By that time I had been covering the Berlin powder-keg for three years, and was familiar with those playing the star roles. Essentially these were Clay's 'political commissar' Robert K. Murphy, who had distinguished himself as a wartime US Consul-General in Algiers by collaborating with a certain Lemaigre-Debreuil, who headed a pro-Nazi French group, in sabotaging the efforts of de Gaulle and the Free French to gain a foothold in North Africa, Brigadier General William H. Draper, the 'economic commissar' and former president of Dillon Read and Company, allied to the Morgan banking empire which helped finance the revival of Ruhr heavy industry after the First World War and was bent on doing the same thing after the Second World War; and the swaggering Texas Cavalry Colonel Frank Howley, limited in everything except his rabid, anti-Sovietism. Howley was the US representative on the four-power *Kommandatura*, or military government of Berlin.

If all this seems far removed from the question of Hiroshima, it was not. Monopoly of the A-bomb had gone to the heads of the American military, affecting their behaviour like hallucinatory drugs. They had gone far beyond the 'implied threat' phase to force the Russians to endorse the repudiation of most of the key clauses of the Potsdam Agreement. And it was an open secret they were itching to use the Bomb against the Soviet Union. General Clay's contribution to Truman's roll-back strategy was known as the 'Task Force Up The Helmstedt Road' project. Helmstedt was a small town on the border of the British and Soviet zones of occupation, seventy miles due west of Berlin, through which the main rail and road traffic passed between the Soviet and Western occupation zones. It might well have become the Sarajevo of World War III.

After a series of US provocations of which I was a personal witness—including the smuggling of Nazi bigwigs to the West, under what was later known as Operation Safehouse—the Russians introduced control measures on their side of the Helmstedt crossing point. The Americans and British could easily have flown these war criminals out from their airfields in West Berlin, and also the former Gestapo agents whom they had recruited to move back and forth between the Soviet and Western occupation zones. But for the deeper reasons of provoking a military showdown with the Russians, they transported them by train in defiance of the original agreements and then insisted on 'no controls'. Traffic ground to a halt. I was aboard the last train—to see for myself the reasons for the Soviet insistence on controls (which I became convinced were more than justified)—before rail and road transport was halted and Clay started his much-publicized 'air lift' to supply the western sectors of Berlin with everything from milk powder to coal for heating. But the real reason was to create a *casus belli* to break what was presented to the western world as the 'Soviet blockade of West Berlin'.

This was the setting for the next phase when a Task Force would shoot its way to Berlin along the Helmstedt-Berlin *autobahn*, and follow-up troops would permanently guard the communication routes. 'Roll-back' would be launched in earnest and, if necessary, any Soviet riposte would receive a crushing nuclear reply. Of course the scheme was not spelt out in such explicit terms. But this secret was ill-guarded from people with access to such men as Clay and Howley in their cups. As Lord Beaverbrook's 'man in Berlin' I had little difficulty in learning the 'scuttlebut' at the American headquarters or receiving 'off-the-record' confidences from US officers.

I communicated my fears, at first in article form to the *Daily Express*, but received a message from Editor Christiansen that while such information was of capital importance it could not be published at that time, but should be relayed to him personally, who would know how best to pass it on to 'higher' levels. As reported earlier, he shared my fears about the likelihood of a nuclear World War III. Beaverbrook, my 'boss' for nine years, although as reactionary as they come, was a complicated character. Once, meeting Christiansen at his editorial office in the famous black glass building in Fleet Street, I was astonished to see behind his chair an almost life-size photograph of Beaverbrook and Stalin embracing each other.

In his capacities as successively Minister of Aircraft Production and Minister of Supply, Beaverbrook twice had to visit Moscow during the War. While the Foreign Office experts spent their time trying to track down prewar contacts, Beaverbrook, on his first visit, immediately sat down with Stalin. Both of them tough, ruthless men of action, they settled everything within a few hours, and then enjoyed themselves at a vodka and caviar session. At a meeting with his staff later that evening, Beaverbrook listened patiently to their activities—who they had seen and who they had not—before saying: 'Well, you can pack your bags and get ready to leave. I've settled everything directly with Stalin.' It was a case of mutual admiration from the moment they met. As a despised colonial, a Canadian, the son of an obscure Presbyterian minister, Beaverbrook was never really accepted by the elite of the British upper class, who regarded him as a 'political adventurer'. They accepted his money for Tory party funds, showered honours upon him, made him a Lord, but he was never really accepted—only tolerated and elevated to high places in desperate moments when his drive and energy were needed. In turn, he never really trusted the Establishment and its minions, many of the latter holding places in Fleet Street. It was one of the reasons why 'The Beaver', as he was known to those who respected him, or 'The Beast' by those who did not, hired many 'colonials', especially Australians, as his star journalists.

At my earlier meeting, when it was decided that I would be reassigned to Germany, Christiansen told me how much 'The Beaver' had been impressed by my Hiroshima report and the initiative I had shown in getting there first, and then said: 'We want you to keep a sharp eye on any trends towards a Nazi revival and that includes any tendency of our own occupation people to be "soft" on the Nazis and "tough" on the Russians.' It was on this basis that I found it possible to cooperate with an ultra-conservative during the first postwar years in Germany. It was the reason also that when 'interdependence' and huge US dollar loans to Britain made it impossible for the *Express* to publish reports critical of American policies in Germany, and Britain's wholesale endorsement of the preposterous American anti-Soviet line and the enlistment of leading Nazi war criminals (like Klaus Barbie) into what was in effect an Allied 'Gestapo', Christiansen was eager to have my private memos. Presumably they were passed on to the 'Beaver-Beast'. Meanwhile, the British had balked—and the French even more so—at the Helmstedt task-force project. They were in no shape to get involved in a shooting war with the Russians, although the Americans pooh-poohed the idea that the Russians would forcibly resist such an incursion. Their rationale was that the Russians were in even poorer shape than the West European allies after their enormous war losses and near famine conditions at home. But as one British officer confided in me: 'The trouble is that the Americans play baseball, the Russians chess. Pity they don't also play cricket. But they're already sowing the whole Helmstedt-Berlin area with mines and Lord knows what sort of booby traps and other obstacles of passive defence. What happens when we get bogged down after the first few hours without the Russkies firing a shot? The French won't have anything to do with it all, neither will the Dutch or other smaller wartime allies. 'Eventually Truman had to take the reluctance his allies into account, especially as it was election season when the scheme was proposed.

However, Clay (who had no battlefield experience) and his political crusaders, were counting on a Dewey victory and a 'green light'. The date for the operation was set for March 1949, by which time Dewey would have supposedly settled in at the White House with John Foster Dulles as his Secretary of State. Just before the election date, Dulles came to Berlin to look things over. He received a group of British correspondents, including myself. Cold and admonitory, he reproached the British for their indecisive attitude. Then came a group from the Congressional Armed Services Committee, headed by Senator Styles Bridges, and including Congressmen Short and Shafer. Leo Muray of the *Manchester Guardian*, Peter Sturzberg of the *Daily Herald* (still the official organ of the British Labour Party in those days) and myself for the *Express* nabbed Short and Shafer as they were going into dinner. They had just come from a top strategy session with Army Secretary Kenneth Royall, Air Force Secretary Stuart Symington, General Walter Bedell Smith, the US ambassador to Moscow (who was shortly to become director of the CIA), and General Lucius Clay. The Committee members had visited Paris and the US occupation headquarters in Frankfurt, where Senator Bridges had remained. The conversation went like this, as I reported it at the time:

'Well gentlemen' said Congressman Shafer, after introductions had been made and he had satisfied himself that we worked for respectable newspapers: 'I don't know that there's very much we can tell you, but shoot away.'

'What impressions did you get from what you have seen and the top level meeting you had today?'

'There's gotta be a showdown with these Russians,' he replied, 'and we're ready to go now. Yes sirs, there's no doubt about it. The longer we wait, the worse things'll get for us. I don't mind telling you boys that we were mighty worried when we left the States, but after what we've seen and heard over here, we're not worried any more. We're ready to go just as soon as they like.'

'Did ambassador Bedell Smith think the Russians were getting ready to move?'

'Well, he wouldn't say that. No sir, he didn't give that impression, but he thinks there's gotta be a showdown alright. And better to have it when we're ready to go, not when they are.'

'But who's going to do the fighting?' Where are you going to get ground troops from?'

'We're not worried about that, not after what we've seen down in the Zone.'

'You mean arm the Germans? You think you can whip the Germans up into an army again?'

Congressman Shafer winked roguishly at his companion: 'Now I don't think we want to say anything about that, do we?' And he answered his own query. 'No, sir, I wouldn't want to tell you anything about that. Of course, you may be sure that's one of the problems we've discussed out here. When we get back to the States we'll draft a report and make certain recommendations to Congress, but I wouldn't want to say what those recommendations would be.'

'General Halder, the former Chief of Staff of the German Army recently made a statement that he was in touch with former officers and could get an army together in no time. Do you think that's correct?'

'Why, certainly. No problem at all. They've got the raw material down there all right. First we've got to get German industry going full blast, and it's well on its way in that direction now.'

'The French have expressed some fears about this revival of German industry; about building up a strong Germany as a base for war. Even General de Gaulle made a pretty strong speech about that a few days ago. He said very plainly that France didn't want a strong Germany. Did you have a chance to go into that aspect while you were in Paris? Won't you have to count fairly heavily on France if this "showdown" comes about?'

At this last question, the roguish look came back into the face of the deputy-chief of the Armed Services Committee, a look which said: 'If only I could tell you poor dopes what's actually going on.'

'You boys', he said, 'can be sure we've taken all that into consideration. The French are being very awkward, that I won't deny. But we figure we can do the job without them. Let them stay out of it. That's all we ask. As long as they stay neutral. At the moment they're saying "No". Just let them stay neutral.... Just stay quiet and we'll do the job alright.'[53]

Of course, the strategists were not worrying about ground troops, except for mopping-up and occupation roles. A few A-bombs would do the trick. Later we read out our notes to Henri de Turenne, then AFP correspondent in Berlin, an ace journalist and today one of France's leading documentary film producers. It made headlines in the French press next day and provoked a mild uproar in the National Assembly. But in general, the whole thing was written off as the ravings of a few garrulous congressmen.

In the end, two things prevented Helmstedt from becoming a nuclearized version of Sarajevo. Against all expectations, Dewey was defeated. If the American flag had been lowered to half-mast at Clay's headquarters, it could not have better expressed the grief and anguish of the A-bomb zealots. The other was that the British under-secretary for foreign affairs was invited to a meeting at the Swiss foreign ministry, at which he was informed that France would have no part in such a military adventure, and the Americans should be told of this—preferably by the British. France's relations with the Americans were so bad that it was 'inconvenient' for them to inform the US authorities directly of this. The British passed it on, adding: 'Of course, with the French taking such a position, we could not possibly...' The Pentagon hawks and their Berlin fledging were left gnashing their beaks over the treachery of their European allies. The 'Helmstedt Task Force' project had to be abandoned. Truman had enough gumption to realize that the United States could not go it alone in such a venture.

After the Berlin crisis calmed down, I moved to Budapest, setting up a base there for travels in other East European countries to see whether the people were counting on their regimes being 'rolled back' *à la* Truman. My firm impression was that they were not, but were hard at work building new societies to replace the old which had irrevocably been swept away. It was while in Budapest that the Korean War broke out and I immediately suspected that what Clay had failed to pull off in Germany, MacArthur—who had no troublesome Occupation Allies to bother about—would pull off in Korea. Not only did MacArthur act independently of any allies, but he also tended to disregard the White House—which is why Truman eventually fired him. It was an extremely grave situation and, as noted in the last chapter, preparations were underway in the United States to make A-bombs feasible for battlefield use. If, in the end, the Americans did not repeat Hiroshima—for a variety of reasons including the development of the Soviet A-bomb and the problem of avoiding incineration of large numbers of their own troops—they did repeat Dresden and Tokyo: firebombing Korea's northern metropolis Pyongyang into flattened rubble that imitated a third 'ground zero'.

Afterword

If the nuclear precipice was narrowly skirted in Berlin in 1948/49 and again in Korea, the close calls had little chastening effect on the American presidency. With a recklessness born of hubris, most of Truman's successors have at one point or another in their administrations recoursed to crude nuclear blackmail: notably Eisenhower in his threats to China over the Formosa Straits in 1957, Kennedy over Cuba in 1962, Nixon during the Yom Kippur War of 1973, and Carter with his Persian Gulf Doctrine of 1979. Now the White House is occupied by a regime which exults in its enthusiasm to make nuclear war 'winnable' and in its willingness to 'go to the brink' over any threatened piece of imperial real estate.

It is a state of affairs endorsed by secrecy and exclusion. As we have seen in the case of the Hiroshima cover-up, censorship and official disinformation have been used since 1945 to blunt public awareness of the consequences of nuclear war and to intimidate the voices of conscience from the *hibakusha*, scientists and servicemen who have dared remind us of the crimes against humanity committed on the 6 and 10 of August 1945. Likewise, from the top-secret beginning of Project Manhattan in 1941, the development of nuclear weapons and strategic nuclear policy have been put above and outside any democratic process. No one in a 'Western democracy' has, in fact, ever voted on the Bomb or its potential use.

In what the Reagan Administration openly trumpets as the 'biggest public relations campaign in history', NATO is currently spending millions to convince us that they are justified in spending thousands of millions to escalate the new cold war. The all-powerful 'Ministries of Truth' are synchronizing the noise-making to drown out the voices from Greenham Common, Central Park and Hiroshima. Many compliant and hungry journalists will undoubtedly be eager to assist this cacophony of official rhetoric. Others, just as undoubtedly, will dissent and attempt to 'get the story right'.

Meanwhile, as the threat of nuclear war increases with each new task force dispatched to a tropical sea, with each Cruise or Pershing missile implanted in Europe, and with each cheer from the sidelines at Westminister and Bonn—we must guard ever more vigilantly against the misapprehension that nothing can be done to stop such a Leviathan in its tracks. Like Eatherly before he became a resister, we are tempted to give way to despair and helplessness. Yet at times like these—most of all—we must take courage and example from the *hibakusha*.

The 'lesson' of Hiroshima is, in my opinion, actually twofold. On the one hand, Hiroshima, like Auschwitz, asserts the existence of a will to genocidal, absolute destruction. We should never cease to meditate on the fact that there has already occurred a first nuclear war, and, because of this precedent, there is little reason to doubt the possibility of a second—particularly if the same constellation of class interests, will-to-power and mind-numbing rhetoric that authorized the exemplary immolation of Hiroshima and Nagasaki is again given pretext and opportunity. On the other hand, Hiroshima also represents the indestructibility of human resistance. Despite their ordeals, the cover-ups, even the ostracism from 'normal' society, the *hibakusha* survivors have fought back, becoming the most stalwart and militant of peaceniks. Through them and their on-going struggle, the *urgency* of Hiroshima is transmitted to all of us.

Notes

1 *New York Times*, 27 March 1983.

2 Hiroshima was, in fact, the headquarters of Japan's Southern Command. It had a garrison headquarters, but otherwise only minor military installations mainly connected with transport.

3 Truman's press statement of 6 August 1945, immediately after the attack on Hiroshima.

4 See *Foreign Relations of the United States*, Diplomatic Papers 1945, Volume VI, Washington D.C. 1969, pp. 472-4.

5 The Committee for the Compilation of Materials on Damage Caused by The Atomic Bombs in Hiroshima and Nagasaki, *Hiroshima and Nagasaki: the Physical, Medical and Social Effects of the Atomic Bombings*, Tokyo 1979 (in Japanese).

6 Doctors Tsuzuki and Miyake are two leading medical specialists well-known for their important publications on the radiation effects of the A-bomb.

7 Refers to George Weller of the Chicago *Daily News*.

8 'Little Boy' was the name supposedly given 'in honour' of Roosevelt while 'Fat Man' was presumably to accord a similar 'honour' to Churchill.

9 *New York Times*, 12 September 1945.

10 I discovered later that this was none other than Brig. Gen. Thomas Farrell, deputy-chief of the Manhattan Project.

11 These were provisional figures given by the police and later revised upwards of 130,000. At the time there was obviously no way of estimating how many victims lay under the ashes nor how many would die soon after from the effects of radiation.

12 *Hiroshima and Nagasaki*, pp. 14-15.

13 Keys was later the Washington bureau chief of UPI for many years, retiring to run the Washington Press Club.

14 *Hiroshima Diary*, translated and edited by Warner Well, Chapel Hill 1965, pp. 209-10.

15 *Ibid*, pp. 228-9.

16 *Ibid*, pp. 81-3.

[17]*Ibid*, pp. 183-5.

[18]Physicians and Scientists on Nuclear War, *The Final Epidemic*, edited by Ruth Adams and Susan Callen, Chicago 1981, pp. 152-3.

[19]*Ibid*, p. 154.

[20]This is blood-chillingly linked to another policy that leading Japanese scientists drew attention to in their massive compilation of materials on Hiroshima and Nagasaki. Apologizing for the still incomplete data on A-bomb damage in their hands even by 1979 when their study was published, the authors wrote: 'The fourth reason for incomplete data on A-bomb damage derives from the restrictions imposed by the Allied Occupation of Japan. On 6 September 1945, the General Headquarters of the Occupation Forces issued a statement that people likely to die from A-bomb afflictions should be left to die. The official attitude in early September was that people suffering from radiation injuries were not worth saving. Then on 19 September, a press code was adopted that imposed prior censorship on all radio broadcasts and on newspapers, magazines and other print media.... As a result, all reports, commentaries and treatises *including even those about treatment of A-bomb related symptoms* were prohibited. Except for a brief time before the press code was imposed, all accounts of A-bomb damages disappeared from newspapers, magazines and academic journals. ... On the other hand, articles that publicized the power of the atomic bomb were warmly welcomed by GHQ....' (*Hiroshima and Nagasaki*, p. 14, my emphasis).

[21]The word *hibakusha* means 'survivor-victims' of the atomic bombs.

[22]*Pikadon* is a composite word in Japanese made up of *pika* to describe a flash like lightning and *don*, a thunderous boom.

[23]*Hiroshima and Nagasaki*, pp. 491-2.

[24]From International Symposium on the Damage and After-Effects of the Atomic Bombing of Hiroshima and Nagasaki, *Proceedings*, published for the National Preparatory Committee by Asahi *Evening News*, 1978, p. 80.

[25]Barton Berstein (ed.), *Politics and Policies of the Truman Administration*, Chicago 1970, p. 32.

[26]*Ibid*, p. 32.

[27]*Ibid*, p. 32.

[28]Marshal Georgi Zhukov, *Reminiscences and Reflections*, Moscow 1971, pp. 92-3 (in Russian).

[29]In *Brighter Than a Thousand Suns*, London 1958, p. 437.

[30]Bernstein, p. 63, footnote 16.

[31]*Inside the Third Reich*, London 1970, pp. 227-8.

[32]*Ibid*.

[33]Jungk, p. 334 (Appendix A), emphasis added.

[34]*Ibid*, p. 175.

[35]*Ibid*, p. 175.

[36]Forrestal later went mad and on 22 May 1949 leapt out of a window of the Bethesda Naval Hospital to his death, believing that he had seen Soviet tanks in the hospital garden.

[37]United States State Department, *Foreign Relations of the United States, Conference on Potsdam,* Vol. VI, p. 876.

[38]*Foreign Relations of the United States, 1945, Far East,* Vol. VI p. 485.

[39]*The Cold War and Its Origins: 1917-1960,* New York 1961, pp. 302-03.

[40]Stanislaw Mikolajczyk headed the London-based Polish government in exile.

[41]Fleming, p. 305.

[42]*Burning Conscience, The Case of the Hiroshima Pilot Claude Eatherly Told In His Letters to Günther Anders,* London 1961, pp. 80-82.

[43]*Ibid,* pp. 80-2.

[44]*New Statesman,* 17 February 1961.

[45]*Atomic Soldiers,* Boston 1981, pp. 2 and 4.

[46]*Ibid,* p. 29.

[47]*Ibid,* p. 30.

[48]*Ibid,* p. 30.

[49]President Reagan's 8 March 1983 speech at Orlando, Florida to the National Associations of Evangelicans was described by the eminent American historian Henry Steele Commanger as the 'worst presidential speech in history—and I've read them all.'

[50]Bernstein, p. 35.

[51]Fleming, pp. 319-20.

[52]For a verbatim transcript of Churchill's speech see *Keesings Contemporary Archives,* pp. 7770-71.

[53]Wilfred Burchett, *Cold War in Germany,* Melbourne 1950, pp. 165-7.